What others are sayi

"Small Change, Big Results *is accessible and engaging, and loaded with examples of how to make changes in your own life. The case studies and stories within are relevant and relatable. Seeing how others have successfully dealt with their issues helps us with our own.*"

– Mai Le, Licensed Marriage and Family Therapist

"*As a business owner, I appreciate the reminder that being productive isn't about being crazy-busy. It's about setting meaningful goals, designing a path to them, and celebrating your successes. This book shows you how to do that with immediate results.*"

– Matt Green, D.C., Village Chiropractic

"Small Change, Big Results *is a must-read for anyone who has struggled with setting and meeting goals. It helps identify the one or two things you can do right away, and guides you to keeping your momentum going forward!*"

– Kay Bosick, Executive Director, Youth and Family Services of Solano County, Inc.

"*Dr. Pat LaDouceur reminds us that success isn't about working harder or faster. This book is an essential guide for anyone who wants to reduce stress and create a happier and healthier life.*"

– Jason Stein, Business Coach, Heart of Business, Inc.

"Pat writes in a clear and conversational way. The examples and snippets of conversation she provides throughout the book model the simplicity of her approach, and make it easy for the reader to use the ideas."

– Lynn Grodzki, Licensed Clinical Social Worker,
Master Coach to Small Businesses

"Following the steps Pat LaDouceur presents in this book will help you get more done with less stress, and enjoy the results. And when you feel good about your own journey, you transfer some of that joy to others in the process. Highly recommended!"

– Catherine Syversen, retired School Administrator

"Sometimes the biggest obstacle to change is our own perception, and if you can change your perception, you can change your circumstances. Small Change, Big Results shows you how to do just that. It's a well-written book by a therapist committed to finding strategies that work."

– Laura Paradise, Life/Career Coach,
Paradise Coaching

small change

BIG RESULTS

*How Simple Actions Can
Reshape Your Life*

Pat LaDouceur, Ph.D.

**Twin Rocks
Press**

Albany, California

small change, **BIG RESULTS**

How Simple Actions Can Reshape Your Life

Pat LaDouceur, Ph.D.

Twin Rocks Press

1505 Solano Avenue, Albany, CA 94707
For Orders and More Information: www.smallchangebigresults.com

ISBN
Paper: 978-0-9906195-0-5
Ebook: 978-0-9906195-1-2

First Edition, 2014
Published in the United States of America

Contact information for resources was accurate at the time of publication, but may have changed since that time. In addition, the author and publisher have no control over the content or functioning of third party websites, and are therefore not responsible for their information, suggestions, or contact information.

Book Design: Peri Poloni-Gabriel, Knockout Design,
www.knockoutbooks.com

Book Editor: Robin Quinn, Brainstorm Editorial,
www.writingandediting.biz

Book Cover Text: Graham Van Dixhorn, Write to Your Market, Inc.,
www.writetoyourmarket.com

Library of Congress Control Number: 2014915492

For Julia, Alex, and Carl,

who encouraged my writing and gave me
the time to put my ideas together

Disclaimer

This book is designed to help you dream big and accomplish your goals. The author's private clients have consistently used these methods to find rewarding work, build caring relationships, and accomplish a variety of personal goals. However, the author and publisher do not have any control over how you use the suggestions presented here, or whether you use them at all. If medical, psychological, financial, or other expert assistance is needed, the services of a competent professional should be sought.

The examples the author uses throughout this book are true, but identifying information has been changed to preserve anonymity. In some cases, the author has combined the stories of several clients so that no actual person can be identified. While not everyone in her practices makes changes as comprehensive as these, the changes are representative of the kinds of things her clients accomplish.

It is not the purpose of this book to gather and summarize all the information that is available on change. You are urged to read all available material, learn as much as possible about habits and change, and tailor the information to your individual needs. For more information, see the many resources at www.smallchangebigresults.com/resources.

There is no promise of instant success. Many of the actions presented here are simple, but that does not always mean easy. Anyone who wants to tackle a difficult or long-standing problem must expect to invest time and effort.

Every effort has been made to make this book as accurate as possible. However, there may be mistakes, both typographical and in content. Therefore this text should be used only as a general guide and not as the ultimate source of information on the process of change. Furthermore, this book contains information that is current only up to the printing date.

The purpose of this book is to educate and entertain. Please use common sense when applying it to your own situation. The author and Twin Rocks Press shall have neither liability nor responsibility to any person with respect to any loss or damage caused, or alleged to have been caused, directly or indirectly, by the information contained in this book.

If you do not wish to be bound by the above, you may return this book to the publisher for a full refund.

"Great things are done by a series of small things brought together."

– Vincent van Gogh

small change, **BIG RESULTS**

How Simple Actions Can Reshape Your Life

COMPLIMENTARY WORKBOOK

All of the exercises in this book are presented in a PDF file with space for your responses, so you'll have a place to record your thoughts and your progress.

Your first simple action is to download your copy at
www.SmallChangeBigResults.com/book.

About the Author

Pat LaDouceur is a licensed Marriage and Family Counselor who helps people become more productive, build rewarding relationships, and enjoy their success. She combines science-based strategies and practical wisdom to help her clients understand the process of change so they can begin to move forward with their goals.

Pat holds a Master's Degree in Clinical Psychology and a Ph.D. in Sociology. She's Board Certified in Neurofeedback, and a former Director of Operations for a non-profit agency.

For the past 27 years, Pat has used the methods presented in this book to help her clients make significant, lasting changes in their relationships, careers and lives.

Pat lives in El Cerrito, California with her husband of 20 years and their teenage twins. She has a private counseling and neurofeedback practice in Albany, CA.

Acknowledgments

Many people have contributed to this book, and it is not possible to mention everyone in this brief section. Still, I would like to thank some of the many people who helped me bring these ideas to the printed page.

I have tried to clarify my own approach while recognizing, being inspired by, and incorporating other approaches. Many thanks to all who have supported this effort.

Many thanks to my editor Robin Quinn at Brainstorm Editorial, whose editorial suggestions made this a far better book. Thanks also to Peri Poloni-Gabriel at Knockout Design for the design of the book cover, and to Graham Van Dixhorn at Write to Your Market for the cover copy.

Many thanks to colleagues, friends, and family who read earlier drafts of the material presented here: Kay Bosick, Silvia Costales, Shannon Dubach, Matt Green, Lynn Grodzki, Janis LaDouceur, Mai Le, Brad Marshland, Susanna Marshland, Carl Mason, Bill O'Hanlon, Laura Paradise, Sojeila Silva, Jason Stein, Catherine Syberson, and Barbara Zuber.

I would like to acknowledge the support of John Eggen and the Mission Marketing Mentors publishing and mentoring program, and of my MMM coach Christy Tryfhus, whose support kept me on track and making steady progress.

My appreciation also goes to my clients, who over the past three decades have shared their mis-steps and successes, and let me know at every step what works and what doesn't.

Contents

Part I:

How Change Works

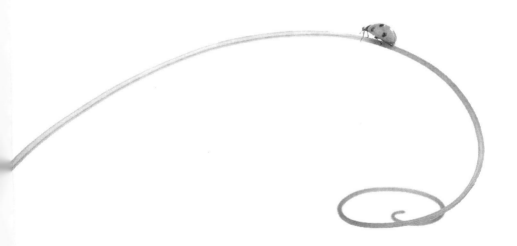

Chapter 1

The Power of Small Change

"They always say time changes things,
but you actually have to change them yourself."

– Andy Warhol

What if you could wave a magic wand and change your life? What would you create? What would make you jump out of bed every day because you were eager to do what you love?

Each year, almost half of the people in the U.S. promise themselves that they will start living differently. Millions of people in the U.S. resolve to improve relationships, reduce stress, save money, land a better job, and get healthy. Many people do indeed make those changes. Most, however, do not.

It's understandable. For one thing, most people are juggling a lot to begin with. It's amazing how difficult life can be at times, and often the effort needed to keep up can leave us feeling anxious, stressed out, overwhelmed, and exhausted! Not only is life becoming increasingly complex and demanding, but it's also flying by at warp speed. It's harder than ever to feel in control.

The pace and complexity of the world we live in affects just about everyone, from business executives to students to professional athletes to stay-at-home parents. Each of us faces a unique set of challenges, fears, and difficult choices, especially in the face of change. Meanwhile, as an old saying goes, constant change is here to stay.

While the pace of life is one reason change is difficult, another problem is equally important: our assumptions about how change works. We admire people who do big things: start successful companies, break athletic records, and triumph over adversity in big ways. These things certainly do deserve admiration. The difficulty comes when we're not able to look behind the scenes at the *process* of change.

Big changes are challenging, right? Well, yes and no. Ultimately it's not the size of the challenge that causes frustration, but rather our perception of it as too big and too complex to manage. This is especially true when we're managing a lot already.

The Essence of Change

The key to making change successfully is understanding how change really works. Over three decades as a counselor, manager, and educator, I've found that there are two key principles of change: (1) Real change is small, and (2) Change creates more change.

Every major change comes from a series of smaller, more manageable steps. No one can "increase sales by 5%" because increasing sales isn't an action. It is possible, however, to make five more phone calls or update a website, and those things might lead to an increase in sales. Phone calls can be broken down into even smaller steps — deciding which people to call, scheduling the time, preparing a sales script, and so forth.

In addition, each small change is like a first domino falling – it provides the *momentum* to make future change more likely. Once you put on your gym shorts, you're more likely to step out the front door. Once you've done that, you're more likely to run – at least down the driveway and back. Once you've started running, you might feel like running just a little farther. When running becomes a routine, you might end up with more energy, which can help you make other changes. One small change builds on another. When you understand these principles, it's possible to get better at the *process* of change.

A Look Forward

In this book, we'll look at challenges we face in our daily lives through the lens of how some people are able to make significant, lasting changes.

The methods presented in *Small Change, Big Results* have helped people become more productive, negotiate tricky work relationships, find their dream jobs, and feel confident enough to start businesses. If you're looking for personal change, the tools and strategies in this book can help you too — from learning to speak confidently, to establishing a healthier life balance, to feeling comfortable in social situations, to improving your relationship with a partner. While the details of each person's journey of change are different, there are familiar patterns that can be teased out and mastered.

In the rest of Part I, we'll take a closer look at why change is so difficult, and begin to consider a winning approach to making it actually happen. In Part II, you'll learn how to use that approach — step-by-step — and it will have you rethinking the process of change. Throughout the book, I'll be sharing stories about the kinds of big results people have accomplished using this process, and you'll see the kinds of small changes they have made to be successful.

Below are three case studies that show some of the challenges people face in the worlds of work and relationships. Alexi was facing problems with productivity and organization that were close to costing her business. Cory was struggling with self-confidence and the stress of an uncertain job future. Sandra was grappling with several major stressors, including a marriage that was on the brink of divorce.

The Stories

When you're listening to someone else's story, it's easy to say, "Well, just change that one thing and your problem will be solved." If only it were so easy!

Maybe you're one of the 50% of people in the U.S. who make New Year's resolutions every year. Unfortunately, only about 12% of those people actually keep their resolutions, while the rest go back to their old habits within days, weeks, or months.[1] Change can be elusive. If diets worked, you'd have already lost the weight, and a lot of weight-loss programs would be out of business. If getting fit were as easy as making a New Year's resolution, you'd have it down by now. There must be something more to change.

Alexi, Cory, and Sandra are smart, skilled, proactive people, committed to solving their problems. They had each tried to get through their situations using problem-solving and willpower. It didn't work.

Their situations were especially tricky for several reasons. First, some aspects of each of their problems were beyond their control. Alexi and Cory were dealing with an unpredictable marketplace, and Sandra with the difficulties of a shared business and the mixed loyalties and angst of her and her husband's teenagers.

Second, Alexi, Cory, and Sandra didn't want just personal change. They also wanted other people to change. Alexi wanted her staff to be more independent. Cory wanted managers to let him work independently on the things he was best at doing. Sandra wanted her husband to quit starting arguments. In this book, you'll see how change evolved for each of these people, step-by-step. At each major junction, we examine the challenges they faced and the solutions they found.

Change can be simple – *if* you understand its essential ingredients. Essentially, in order to change, you need to understand both the problem itself and what's driving it – the thoughts, feelings, assumptions, and not-so-obvious triggers that are just below the surface. Right now, let's learn a little more about Alexi, Cory, and Sandra.

Alexi's Story: *Low Productivity and "Crazy Busy"*

Alexi sat down heavily on my office couch. "I can't focus at work," she said. "I work twelve-hour days, but I don't get done what other people do in eight. And my income depends on what I accomplish, so I'm not making half of what I should. Saving is out of the question. At this rate, I'll have to work until I'm ninety."

Alexi was a smartly dressed financial advisor. She'd only been in business for two years. But there was no reason, Alexi said, that she shouldn't be able to make her business work. Her colleagues respected her, and her staff and two interns gave her glowing reviews. Her mentors were encouraging, and a little puzzled.

Alexi had been diagnosed with Attention Deficit Disorder (ADD) 8 months earlier, and she had been taking stimulant medication ever since. It didn't seem to be enough.

"I still have trouble getting things done," Alexi explained. "There's a lot to running a business – loads of little tasks. Other people depend on me, and they have questions. By the time I get to the important stuff, I can't focus."

"How have you handled the problem so far?" I asked.

"Longer hours," she said. Alexi got to her office about 7:30 a.m. and left at 7:00 p.m. She originally took work home occasionally just to catch up. However, like many people, her evening work turned into a habit and her "to do" list remained long. Despite this strategy's lack of success, she continued to wake up at 5:30 a.m. to be at the office early.

When you're in the middle of "crazy busy," it's hard to see solutions. Willpower didn't work for Alexi. Putting in more time only made her more exhausted. She thought about changing careers, moving to the country, or perhaps winning the lottery. Realistically, Alexi didn't have a plan, but she was committed enough to take action – if only she could figure out what action to take.

Cory's Story: *Worry and Internal Stress*

Cory, too, was worried about work. He had a well-paid position as a software developer at a mid-sized computer technology company. He'd found the job in his late twenties. Cory had worked on various projects at the same organization for more than 6 years, an unusual feat in a field with high job turnover.

Although his position seemed relatively safe, Cory worried about the unpredictability of his profession. As new technology is developed, large numbers of people are hired and then laid off. Companies emerge, then merge and disappear, or are bought out. Funding falls through; cuts are made. Any of these things, Cory thought, could happen to him. That kind of thinking kept him up at night.

Cory wasn't alone in feeling stressed out by work. In fact, stress is the number one problem reported by both business owners and employees. Stress takes a toll on physical and emotional energy, as well as relationships.

Citing a number of other studies, a 1995 report by the Centers for Disease Control states that for a quarter of all employees, work is life's number one stressor.[2] Forty percent of workers say their job is "very or extremely stressful." Twenty-six percent of workers say they are "often burned out or stressed by their work." These stresses are accompanied by health, family, and financial problems.

In a more recent 2012 report, the picture looks even worse. Eighty-three percent of workers are experiencing job stress. Stressors include not only the possibility of job loss, but also an unreasonable work load, a difficult boss or colleague, long commutes, and poor work-life balance.[3]

Cory had another worry as well. His programming skills were solid, but coding took up only about a third of his time. Over the years, his job had changed from one that was solitary, and suited his personality well, to one that was fairly social. Cory spent much of his time with difficult clients and quirky managers. He was seen as a resource by some of his newer colleagues – a testament to his knowledge, but a strain on his rather shy temperament. He felt out of his element in large team meetings and uncomfortable making presentations to clients.

Cory wanted to reduce his level of stress. He wanted to stop worrying about things that *might* happen and to feel more comfortable with social interactions at work. He wanted to enjoy the people he liked and feel more confident with those who were more difficult.

For people who struggle with anxiety, the challenge is to learn to change not only their feelings and physiological response, but also the anxious thoughts that are driving that response. On a practical level, Cory needed to move out of his communication comfort zone.

Relationships, by definition, involve more than one person, but it's amazing how much one person's change can shift communication patterns. Finding the right strategies, however, takes some experimenting. Our path through change involved doing just that.

Sandra's Story: *Relationship Change*

"If you can't help us, we're getting divorced." Those were Sandra's first words when she and her husband Jay sat down in my counseling office.

Sandra and Jay had known each other for almost a decade, and they had been married for four years. They each had children from a prior marriage: Sandra, a 16-year-old daughter, and Jay, 15- and 17-year-old sons. Their lives were more intertwined than those of most married couples, because they ran a business together. The business started as a project they could share, but had steadily become a major source of stress.

Spouses working together can be rewarding when done well – when the partners create a joint mission, detailed written business plan, and clear roles. Of course, creating these things takes time and excellent communication skills, two things Sandra and Jay didn't have. Because this foundation wasn't in place, they struggled with not only the stress of owning a new and struggling company, but also their hard-to-negotiate differences in preference and style. They both worked long hours for little income.

On top of that, blended families have their own sets of stresses, including mixed loyalties, questions about which parent is in charge, and children's feelings about living with people they didn't grow up with. Since finances were tight, the five of them shared a small, three-bedroom house, and the small space increased the tension. Breakfast time was a free-for-all as each person tried to get ready for school or work. Dinner time was nonexistent, since they each came and went at different hours. Since there was no coordinated plan for chores, the majority of them fell on Sandra.

The worst part for Sandra, though, was the constant disagreeing between her and Jay. It seemed like anything, no matter how large or small, was enough to start another round of complaint, criticism, or period of silence. Change was needed on many levels, but their problems seemed so many and so complex that Sandra and Jay didn't know where to start. They had all but given up.

At best, relationships are antidotes to stress. A Turkish proverb claims, "No road is long with good company." Most studies on happiness find that happy marriages and close friendships predict personal well-being. For this reason, Sandra, Jay, and I focused first on their relationship, so that it could become a support instead of a source of stress. Their marriage relationship is the part of their efforts to change that we'll follow in this book. The three of us worked together much of the time, but for the sake of simplicity I'll focus mostly on Sandra's efforts. 🖋

Big Results from Small Change

The results experienced by each of these clients were big. Alexi took her business from struggling to successful in less than a year. In the same time period, Cory stopped trying to avoid change, and he stepped outside of his comfort zone in a way that led him toward a leadership position. Sandra changed almost every part of her life over a period of about 2 years. She healed her marriage, facilitated family cooperation, got back into shape, helped sort out her and Jay's joint business, and started doing some of the graphic design work she loved.

Other clients, who you'll also meet in these pages, were able to start an exercise program, get over a fear of heights, land an excellent job, and start writing short stories.

How were these people able to get results? And if the changes were based on actions that were "simple," why weren't they able to make the same changes years earlier?

There are a couple of reasons for this. First, it's not always easy to identify the *root cause* of the problem. For example, Alexi's push to put in long days "for a while" to catch up didn't address a key issue: her brain-based difficulty with attention and focus due to the ADD and the external supports and structure she needed to compensate for this. Because the solutions she tried addressed only the main *symptom*, her business continued to struggle.

Second, none of us operates alone. The solutions you attempt to apply affect (and are affected by) other people and circumstances. Turning around a relationship or an organization is a bit like changing the course of a large ship. Attempts at big change are often met by equally strong forces that counter the change. If this "push-back" is not taken into account, one person's new actions won't *seem* to matter much, and there is a tendency to give up too soon. Sandra, for example, wanted to change her relationship with her husband and his children. Any change, ironically even *positive* change, was likely to result in push-back from those people.

On the other hand, a barely noticeable small change at sea can make the difference between whether your ship ends up in Florida or New York. In the same way, a small change in your life can make a big difference in the results you get.

One of the keys is to make the changes small. Small change doesn't exhaust you, nor does it create much push-back. Instead, small change sets in motion a very different force. When you make space for your priorities, you free time and mental space for things that nourish you and help you relax. This reduces stress, improves productivity, and creates space for enjoyment and happiness. All of this contributes to feeling more positive about the overall process of change.

Alexi, Cory, and Sandra are the kinds of people I work with every week. Their stories are based on the stories of actual clients, with identifying details changed to preserve privacy. I'll refer back to them throughout this book, so you can see some of the roadblocks they encountered and how they got past them. I'll introduce other people as well, so you'll have a variety of examples to choose from for inspiration and ideas as you navigate your own process of change.

Looking back, the changes they made seem broad and sweeping. However, the real changes were small. For example, week by week, Sandra and Jay committed to simple actions that led them in the direction of the relationship they wanted. Each tiny action gave this couple hope and motivation, which inspired them to try another small change. In the end, the result was sweeping.

This type of successful change is possible for you too. You can find the work you love, build rich, rewarding relationships, create a legacy, or anything else you desire through a process of simple, focused action.

If you've already tried to change but had trouble making it "stick," there's a good chance you'll recognize some of the obstacles described in Chapter 2. In it, we'll look at why, despite our best intentions, it seems so hard to change even the smallest details of our lives.

Chapter 2

Why Most Resolutions Fail

*"Most people are so busy knocking themselves out
trying to do everything they think they should do, they never
get around to what they want to do."*

– Kathleen Winsor

What's the difference between people who say they want to change and people who actually do change? Eighty-eight percent of all New Year's resolutions set by people in the U.S. fail, according to researcher Richard Wiseman.[1] This happens despite the fact that people try an average of 10 times to make their resolutions work.[2]

However, 12% of resolution-makers succeed, and psychologists have been trying to understand how they do it. There is, in fact, a growing science of change, which is beginning to help us understand exactly how we can make lasting adjustments to our lives. It turns out, for example, that change isn't just one thing. Every significant change is really *a sequence of tiny events.*

In addition, within that sequence are very specific places where it's easy to get distracted or diverted. If you understand the predictable ways this happens, it's much easier to make the changes you want.

Have you ever promised yourself that you'd catch up with your email, only to find the same backlog the next day? Ever sign up for a gym membership and then make it to just a few workouts? Or maybe you promised yourself to be more patient with your kids, and you still ended up losing it. If the change you want isn't happening, you've probably encountered one of these seven common barriers to change:

1. You're "crazy busy."

2. Your heart isn't in it.

3. You don't have a plan.

4. You rely too much on willpower.

5. You misunderstand motivation.

6. You run into trouble – and don't persist.

7. You don't recognize success.

Let's look at these barriers one at a time.

1. You're "Crazy Busy"

Have you ever found yourself saying things like...

+ "Sorry, don't have time!"

+ "I'm swamped."

+ "Can't seem to catch up."

+ "I'm overbooked."

+ "I feel so underwater!"

If these comments sound familiar to you, you're in good company. No matter what form your work takes, it's easy to get overly busy. If you're running a business, the success of the company depends on your direction. If you're a professional, you want to do your best work – and there's probably a lot of it. If you're self-employed, your financial survival depends on your efforts. Stay-at-home moms have their hands full with children and chores.

In addition, there are other types of commitments to friends, family, and partners. Even if the relationships are a joy, all these connections tug on your time.

In response to the pressures, a common approach is to try to work harder, or bank on being more efficient. Learning to be efficient is a worthy cause, and with a few simple tools, most people can significantly increase their efficiency. However, "doing more" is *not* one of these tools. As soon as you make progress by working harder, you get more ideas, requests, and assignments. Unless you change the structure of your day, the systems you use, and the process by which you make decisions, catching up can be difficult to impossible.

No one's energy is infinite. "Solutions" like bringing work home and working on the weekends "just to get caught up" can easily turn into a new routine – and one that's hard to get out of. Expectations increase, and eventually you're known as the person who gets things done – at the expense of personal time, lunch breaks, exercise, and healthy food. With less self-care, you end up being more tired and less able to prioritize and plan. You end up in another busy cycle.

Doing too much, even of the "right" things, can make it harder to reach your dreams and goals. It's not *how much* you do that makes a difference, but rather which choices you make and how you manage your energy. In a burst of enthusiasm, you tell yourself that this is the weekend to clean off your desk and sign up for the gym. But you already have a report due at work on Tuesday and a phone meeting on Saturday as treasurer for the PTA. What gets lost? The Friday night movie with your husband? The Saturday morning walk with your son?

In a couple of surveys, psychologists Philip G. Zimbardo and John N. Boyd found that the biggest toll of being busy is on *relationships* and *well-being*. When pressed for time, about 30% of people give up time with family, 44% see less of friends, 56% get less sleep, and 57% give up hobbies. Only 6% decide to work less. At the same time, 40% of the respondents said that lack of time caused stress in their relationships.[3]

One reason *busy* is so compelling is that it looks normal. It seems that *everyone's busy*. How many times have you run into a friend on the street and apologized for not keeping in touch with a conversation like this:

You: "Silvia, it's so great to see you. Sorry I haven't been in touch, but I've been so busy!"

Silvia: "Oh, no problem, I've been swamped myself. Let's get together soon, okay?"

Busy serves as reassurance that you and Silvia still care about each other. You haven't been in touch for reasons "beyond your control" – that is, *busyness*. Being busy is a ready-made excuse and at the same time a way to connect.

Because busy seems so normal, interruptions have become part of daily life. It's hard to resist them. Our response to them is strong and outside of our awareness, and the added demands add to our busyness. Yet in a way these interruptions are comfortable, because they are familiar. Resisting them takes awareness, focus, and energy.

Exercise 2.1

· ·

Review the list below to see how much being "crazy busy" is keeping you from living the life you want. Each statement is a version of doing more, or of working faster and harder. When you're finished, write the total number of "yes" responses on a designated legal pad or in the complimentary Small Change, Big Results Workbook. *The maximum number of possible "yes" responses is 14.*

The "Crazy Busy" Scale

+ I often work later than I plan or want to work.

+ Most nights, I take work home.

- It's not unusual for me to go back to work after dinner.
- I work at least one weekend a month.
- My "to do" list grows faster than I can finish the items on it.
- I take on projects I'd rather not do.
- I take on projects I don't have time for.
- I make lists to keep track of my other lists.
- I never feel "finished" for the day.
- I spend a lot of time working in "crisis mode."
- I get more done by cutting back on sleep.
- I'm too busy to spend the time I'd like with my family.
- I'm too busy to spend the time I'd like with my friends.
- I've given up meaningful hobbies because I'm too busy to fit them in.

If you've said "yes" to even a few of these items, it's time to think about how to slow down to a pace of life you can sustain. If you've checked six or more, you're "crazy busy" and in serious danger of burn-out. This book will show you how to regain balance.

. . . .

2. Your Heart Isn't in It

Your goal has to *matter* – not just theoretically, but in your gut. It needs to be anchored in your values – the guiding principles that you use to make choices and decisions throughout your life. These are the big, hard-to-describe things that matter most, like adventure, financial security, generosity, and leadership – the qualities that have the most meaning for you. Your values give you the energy, commitment, and persistence to move forward – not only when the path is smooth, but also when you're knee-deep in mud and scrambling over rocks.

It's surprising how hard we sometimes try for things we don't care much about. My client Tonya, for example, was looking for work. Her primary values were about relationships, and yet she was looking for jobs in a highly structured business environment. She thought those places would be a good match for her financial skills. Yet she was dragging her feet at every step of the search process.

Once Tonya understood the mismatch – that her role at the larger firms would likely be disconnected from the organization's day-to-day operations, she began to look at smaller social services agencies. She found several mission-focused agencies where she could easily see herself as part of the agency's commitment to helping people. Only then was she able to regain her confidence and momentum. She found a well-paid position within three months.

Values affect not only the type of work you do, but also how you spend your money, what you do for fun, and the kind of people you attract. When a new behavior is connected to your values, it becomes more compelling than the behavior you currently have.

For example, Anna wanted to lose weight because she wanted to love the way she looked. However, she had struggled with this goal for decades with only intermittent success. Anna had a loving relationship and satisfying work, so beyond Anna's feelings about her appearance, the weight didn't seem to be affecting her in any other way. This changed when she got an unfortunate medical diagnosis, which was connected her to a primary value of health. Her goal had suddenly become relevant. The extra weight came off in six months, and stayed off.

Exercise 2.2

Look over the List of Values and choose four or five that resonate with you the most. Feel free to also consider values that aren't on this list. List them on a designated notepad or in the Workbook, so you can refer back to them throughout this book. As you move through the change process, these will be your anchors.

List of Values

Adventure	Freedom	Learning
Commitment	Fulfilling work	Legacy
Compassion	Fun	Love
Cooperation	Generosity	Loyalty
Creativity	Hard work	Passion
Curiosity	Health	Practicality
Education	Honesty	Relationship
Empathy	Humility	Service
Faith	Intelligence	Spontaneity
Family	Joy	Teamwork
Financial security	Leadership	Travel

Values can change over time as your life changes. Parents, for example, often shift their values from autonomy to family once their children are born. Thus it's worth re-considering your values from time to time and thinking about how they affect your choices and actions.

Here's a possible guideline for making sure your heart is in any new project you take on. Ask yourself if the change is something you want, instead of something you should do. "I should get in shape" might become "I want to feel healthy and full of energy." "I should do my homework" might change to "I want to learn biology so I'll do well in medical school." Important life decisions have to come from careful thought and from your own heart.

3. You Don't Have a Plan

Once you connect with your values and begin to imagine a goal you love, it's tempting to jump right in and get started. "I'm going to take care of my finances," you declare in a burst of enthusiasm. However, you probably won't follow through –unless you have a clear plan to make it happen, including some steps along the way.

To reach a goal, you need a map. Without one, you'll end up either responding to the most urgent problem, or spending too much mental energy keeping track of unrelated details. When that happens, your day tends to be filled by crisis and random events, and it's unclear what to do first. That report is due next week – do you need to work on it today, or can you wait until tomorrow? A colleague wants help with a project. Do you have time to get involved? What will you have to give up in order to help her?

Unless the details of your vision have been clearly thought through, the answers to the questions in the last paragraph can easily be "I don't know." Decisions get made based on urgency and mood, important details are left until the last minute, and a few things slip through the cracks.

When you have a plan, your mind is free to wander down more creative and more productive paths. Within a structure, your mind is free to roam.

One talented art teacher I know taught every 12-year-old student in her class to draw a realistic portrait. Portraits are hard to draw, because our minds are so full of ideas about what faces *should* look like that it's hard to see what they *do* look like. One of the things this teacher was so good at was mapping out the process for her students. She was able to tell them where to start, how to look, when to focus on the big picture and when to look at the details. In short, she had created a step-by-step plan to help students move toward their goal. Every student's project looked like a real person. The structure she provided gave them a skill, and it brought out their creativity.

Plans are also an antidote to worry. When you don't plan ahead, you're often forced to "wing it" – and can end up worried. Worry, in turn, interferes with the ability to come up with creative solutions to the real obstacles you face. It's not enough to plan how to avoid problems, although it is helpful to do so. It's even more important to plan what you'll do if you have to face them.

When the pressure is on, without a plan, we revert to our usual way of doing things. Let's look at Alexi, for example, the financial advisor from Chapter 1. Even when Alexi was clear about how she wanted her business to look, she found it hard to change her habits. Each time she tried to change her workday, her efforts lasted for only a few days. Once she had a plan, Alexi was able to make the changes stick.

4. You Rely Too Much on Willpower

Interestingly, change can still be tricky – even when you know exactly what you want and you've thought through a clear way to get there. Consider these examples:

+ I'm going to make 40 client calls every weekday.
+ I'm going to spend every Friday night with my family.
+ I'm going to run three times a week starting Tuesday morning.
+ I'm going to lose 20 pounds by the end of June.

These goals are good ones. They're specific, measurable, reasonable, and they have a clear time frame. All you need is a little willpower, right?

If you want to create something that will last, you have to build it on stable ground. Otherwise, like with the leaning Tower of Pisa, things will go awry. Using willpower to ensure lasting change is problematic, because willpower isn't sustainable. It takes energy, both physical and mental, and that energy gets used up during the course of your day.

When you do something that's not part of your regular routine, your brain uses energy. As you go through your day making choices and ignoring distractions, that energy is consumed. Physically, you can feel depleted. Mentally, you'll find it harder to focus and make decisions.

Under stress, this process happens more quickly. Once your energy stores are depleted, it's much easier to go back to your usual habits.

In their book *Willpower,* psychology professor Roy Baumeister and his co-writer John Tierney cite studies suggesting that we spend about a quarter of our days resisting desires – and we're successful at resisting them only about half the time.[4] This means that when you take on a new challenge, you're already under some "willpower strain."

In addition, you probably don't have an extra hour in your schedule readily available to make calls or get more exercise. That leaves only two ways to include the new behavior in your schedule: (1) stop doing something else in order to make room for it; or (2) add it into your schedule and hope things somehow sort themselves out. Since the former requires a decision (and willpower), most people end up doing the latter – it's the easiest *short run* decision.

In the long run, though, you end up with too much on your plate. In her book *The Willpower Instinct,* author Kelly McGonigal argues that "trying harder" to create change doesn't work. It's too easy to *overestimate* your energy and *underestimate* the pull of your existing routines. Both of these misestimations often result in overtaxing your willpower and ultimately in abandoning your new goal.[5]

Although it's unreliable, willpower can be one of our greatest assets, and successful people know how to use it to accomplish their goals. As you read through this book, you'll learn how they do it.

5. You Misunderstand Motivation

Do any of these excuses sound familiar?

- ✦ "I need to exercise, but I'm not motivated."
- ✦ "I can't motivate myself to write today."
- ✦ "I just can't stay focused on this project."

Most people think of motivation as something that's beyond their control. If you're lucky, you feel motivated – otherwise you struggle.

Some of the misunderstanding comes from confusing motivation with inspiration. Inspiration is a feeling of excitement, which happens especially when something is fun, new, or creative. It's usually easier to find inspiration at the beginning of projects or in the imagining process – before the project is fully formed. That initial excitement is part of motivation, but motivation is much more. In essence, motivation is a *willingness* to do something. It comes from a particular combination of inspiration, routine, and environment.

My client Laura, for example, told me that she wasn't motivated to write. However, writing was Laura's livelihood and her passion. "I started writing fiction when I was seventeen," she told me, "and I felt like I was living my dream." A few years later, she ran straight into writer's block. For a writer, she explained, this is one of the worst things that can happen. Writers and performers often rely on inspiration on a daily basis. They're always on the lookout for something fresh and new, and when that creative flow is blocked, it's a problem.

"I don't feel inspired these days," Laura told me. "I don't like what shows up on the paper. I stare at it for a while, then give up and tell myself I'll try again tomorrow. But the same thing happens the next day." She hadn't produced a sentence she liked for months.

Laura was waiting to feel motivated, but feelings are by nature fleeting.

Fortunately, motivation isn't something you're either lucky enough to have or you have to live without, but rather something you *can* create. We'll look more at how you can create motivation in Chapter 8, "Act."

When Laura learned to create her own motivation, she was much less at the mercy of her moods. After that, the right words began to come to her once again.

6. You Run into Trouble – and Don't Persist

Obstacles are part of the territory. If your goal really matters, you're likely to encounter challenges. These challenges can distract, dissuade, and divert you from your path, no matter how solid your intentions.

Sometimes you can make a quick adjustment and get back on your path. At other times, you can easily find yourself on unfamiliar ground.

Obstacles might be real *external events*. Maybe you don't get the job you wanted, you twist your ankle, or you run out of money before a project is finished. Or maybe the problem is a more serious economic setback or natural disaster.

Obstacles can also be *internal* – the stories you tell yourself about an event: "I really blew it" or "The job was too hard" or "I never liked writing anyway. I'm not good at it." Or the thoughts might be about the world around you: "There aren't any jobs out there because the economy is bad" or "No one wants to hire teachers/contractors/economists." These inner voices are your own, and when times get rough, you might be tempted to believe them.

Sometimes other people add their voices to these internal ones, and in the cacophony, it's hard to hear your own inner wisdom. Negative thoughts create feelings like worry, frustration, fear, and doubt. Then you're not only looking for ways around external obstacles, you're also struggling with these internal ones as well. The boulders on the road can seem enormous.

But as Einstein said, "Anyone who has never made a mistake has never tried anything new." Mistakes, wrong guesses, failed experiments, and disappointments are part of change. They're not indicators of a flaw in your plans; they're part of life. The secret is remembering that obstacles are part of the terrain and knowing how to get back on your own path with a minimum of drama.

Rayna, for example, was passed over for a promotion in favor of a young man who'd spent much less time at her company. She knew she had the skills to do the job, but didn't want to create bad will by protesting the decision. She thought the problem might be sexism.

Most of the time, there's a way around an obstacle, no matter how daunting it seems – as it did feel at first to Rayna. In the long run, though, Rayna was able to change her situation by being clear, thoughtful, and assertive. She was able to educate her supervisors about her value to the organization, and by doing so, she paved the way for several other women to advance along with herself.

Sometimes reaching your goal is simply a matter of *continuing to try*. As Benjamin Franklin said, "Energy and persistence conquer all things." Persistence isn't just about willpower – it's about taking one simple, thoughtful step after another to find your way past obstacles.

One woman, Loreen Niewenhuis, did this literally. She walked a thousand miles, or about 5,280,000 steps, around Lake Michigan, and chronicled her path in a memoir. It took her 64 days of walking over footpaths and sandy beaches, as well as around rocks and through rough neighborhoods.[6] Five million steps take persistence!

Author Malcolm Gladwell suggests that it takes something like 10,000 hours to become an elite performer, to master computer programming, or to perform any other skill extremely well.[7] The ability to take one step after another is as important as talent.

Fortunately, you can learn to feel confident in the face of challenges. Confidence is largely about mindset – what you tell yourself about the challenge, about success and failure, and about yourself. Learning to change your mindset is a key part of the path to successful change.

7. You don't recognize success

At the end of the day, which of these thoughts is closer to what you're thinking?

+ I got seven things done today. That's fabulous!

+ I got seven things done today, but I have 3,941 things left to do. I'm not getting anywhere.

The first thought is worth celebrating; the second one clearly isn't. Either way, you finished seven things. The difference is in how you view what you did. With the first thought, there is a sense of accomplishment, and in the second, a sense of resignation and overwhelm. "I'll celebrate when I finish," you tell yourself, but when will you finish? At the end of one project, there are three others you've put on hold. The process is never-ending.

In a race, there is a tendency to focus on the finish line. However, in reality, it's not just the last step that's important. Each step along the way helped get you there.

There's a temptation to minimize the impact of what you do. "I unpacked one box, but I have a whole house to organize," you might say. Or perhaps, "I wrote a sentence, but so what? I have a whole chapter to write." There is a criticism, a put-down in those words, and it's hidden in the word "but."

It's true that you've unpacked one box. It's also true that you have a whole house to organize. Those two things are connected in the long run, if you've planned well. In the short run, however, the latter is irrelevant.

"That's nothing" you might tell yourself after finishing one paragraph of a novel. But if that paragraph was difficult to write, this kind of self-talk can undermine you. Imagine running a marathon and at every step telling yourself, "I've only run a mile, hardly anything. I'll never finish at this rate." With that kind of self-talk, you never would.

When you don't value your own effort, energy, and hard work, it's hard to keep going. You start to feel like you're not getting anywhere, and feel like giving up. Of course it's possible that you really are sliding back into your old routine. But it's also possible that you're making exactly the kind of progress you need to heal your relationship, complete the project, or organize the house. In this book, you'll learn to recognize that and give yourself credit.

Exercise 2.3

Have you ever made a resolution, only to abandon it in the following days, weeks, or months? If so, what got in the way of your sticking with it?

Exercise 2.4

Have you ever made a resolution and stuck with it? What did you have to do to make that happen? What inspired you? What obstacles did you overcome? How did you celebrate your success?

Exercise 2.5

Think of one to three resolutions you have made recently, or would like to make, and write them down on a notepad or in the Small Change, Big Results Workbook. You'll be able to translate them into actions as you go through the steps outlined in this book.

If you've encountered any of the stumbling blocks described in this chapter, know that many others have too. It's no surprise that most resolutions fail, and that so many people get frustrated and feel like giving up.

Fortunately, there is a way through. Study after study has shown that there are definite, predictable ways that people can successfully change their habits, thought patterns, and circumstances. No matter how busy you are or how frustrated you've felt, change *is* possible. The path to change is outlined next, in Chapter 3.

Chapter 3

How People Change

"The principal activities of brains are making changes in themselves."

– Marvin Minsky (from *The Society of Mind*)

There are reliable steps in the process of change. I've observed them with my clients over the past 27 years. There are seven that I have identified as crucial: *pause, imagine, plan, shrink, act, flow, and celebrate.* In *Small Change, Big Results,* I'll explain why each one is important, how it works, and how you can incorporate it into your own life to find work you love, rejuvenate your relationships, and improve your health.

These steps build on each other, and for most people, it's best to read through them in order, beginning with Chapter 4, "Pause." However, if you're curious about one of the steps and want to jump ahead, that's fine too. Whichever you do, make sure that for each step you *take action.* You'll find exercises in each chapter to help you to more easily incorporate the steps into your life.

Pause

The first step in creating change is to *pause* – to take a few minutes each day to renew your energy, sharpen your focus, and reflect on how you use your time. A pause is an antidote to "crazy busy," because it helps you slow down and make room for the people and activities you care about most.

The most important reason, though, is that learning to pause *changes the way you think about time*. With time to reflect, you'll find it easier to focus on your priorities, and you'll start to plan your days differently.

Most people realize that time for reflection and renewal is beneficial. However, relatively few people end up making that time happen. It's easy to put off breaks, vacations, personal time, and even sleep until "tomorrow."

In Chapter 4 ("Pause"), you'll learn more about how unstructured time can make you more productive, why taking that time seems so difficult, and how to build relaxation and reflection into your own life. You'll learn how changing the way you use time can help you reduce stress, slow the pace of your life, and relax physically and mentally. We'll look at how and when you can build in both stress-reducing activities and time off.

Each of my clients from Chapter 1 found that by slowing down, they were able to make changes that had otherwise eluded them. Alexi needed a few minutes at the beginning of her day to reflect on her priorities. When Alexi added this to her routine, she gained new perspective and was able to make changes. Cory was able to counter his worry by learning to consciously relax at the beginning and end of his day. Over time, this change helped him let go of worry, improve his sleep, and stay calm in difficult situations. For Sandra, family time was her top priority. She eventually found a way to spend fun, quality time every day with the people she cared about most.

Imagine

Imagination is the second step in creating change, and it's discussed in Chapter 5. When you create new images and reinforce them, you develop new neural networks[1] (a process discussed at the end of this chapter) and your brain changes. While creating a clear, mental picture of what you want doesn't guarantee positive results, it does make them much more likely.

Over time, imagining can help you create in your life almost anything you want. Great athletes and performers know that imagining the result they want makes the difference between creating something meaningful, and drifting toward whatever happens next. Hundreds of studies over the past 30 years have shown that imagination is supremely practical. In the forms of envisioning, mental rehearsal, active imagination, and other practices, imagination helps with healing, creativity, optimal performance, and reaching goals.[2] It turns out that in many circumstances, the brain can't tell the difference between mental and physical reality.

Let's look at the role imagination played for one of my clients. Sandra's challenge was significant. She wanted to heal her marriage, which meant changing some deeply embedded communication patterns. Her arguments with Jay were fueled by some very real life pressures – a blended family, financial stress, a too small living space – and by emotions that were hard to talk about. Instead of turning to each other for support, those stressors were driving a wedge between Sandra and Jay.

One of the first things I asked Sandra to do was to imagine the relationship she wanted, in vivid detail. She ended up with a vision of not only how Jay would show his caring and affection, but how she would act, what she would say, and how she would feel. The images she chose provided the inspiration and energy Sandra needed to make new choices every time she and Jay talked.

Because of her crystal-clear vision of the desired changes in the relationship, and her determination to put her vision into practice, her relationship started to shift. Within weeks, the arguments disappeared. In less than a month, she and Jay were spending relaxed, enjoyable time together. Over a period of about six months, Sandra made significant changes in her parenting, leisure time, and work, all inspired by her vision of what was possible.

Imagining is only part of the story, but it often creates a turning point. Of all the possible paths you could travel, you can choose one that is the most inspiring, most compelling, and most meaningful – a path that connects with your values, your dreams, and your sense of purpose. Imagining what truly matters to you is the essence of a powerful goal.

Plan

Planning is where you transform carefully imagined goals into real, doable ones. It's a way of turning an inspiring image into a series of thoughtful actions.

Plans give form to your dreams. If imagining shows you what the treasure is, then planning is your map. Like all good maps, your plan gives you a good sense of the terrain you'll encounter. But it's different from a real map in one important way – you adjust your plan as you go. Your path will be, to some extent, unpredictable, and a good plan allows room for that unpredictability.

Chapter 6 ("Plan") shows you how to plan effectively. In this chapter, you'll learn how to stay connected to your vision and priorities, so you don't end up single-mindedly pursuing your ideal job but neglecting your family. You'll learn to identify milestones, so you can tell when you're making progress. You'll see the importance of including unscheduled time in your plans, and how to deal with the randomness that inevitably creeps into your day. Most importantly, you'll learn to choose effective next steps so you reach your goals as efficiently and enjoyably as possible.

Let's look at "Will I have enough money to retire?" A first-draft plan might look like this: (1) Decide how and where I want to live; (2) Decide how much I need per month to retire by reading books on retirement planning or consulting a professional; (3) Look at my current budget and savings pattern and see if I'm on track (if I'm not sure, get help or do more research); (4) If I'm on track, great, and if I'm not, I need a plan to match up my savings/spending patterns and retirement goals. Once you make this plan and follow it, no more worry!

One of Alexi's goals was to leave work at work, so she could enjoy her evenings and bring back her social life. Alexi knew that to change this, she would have to adjust not only some of her own habits, but also some of the habits and expectations of others.

Alexi's plan helped her schedule her most difficult work at times when she had the most energy. With this in mind, she was able to both catch up on projects and build her business by focusing on the details that mattered most. Within two weeks, she had free time. In four months, she had taken care of her backlog of work. In less than a year, she had a financially successful business. This happened because at every step, Alexi knew exactly what to do next.

Alexi's original vision of evenings with friends was powerful, but the path to get there wasn't clear. A plan created a way to make her intention concrete, and it helped her find the first step. The plan was the link between her dream and her ability to take small, steady steps toward accomplishing the goal.

Shrink

Once you have a plan in place, you'll find that small change leads to surprisingly big results. Most of the time, small change is more effective than big change. This is true for several reasons. First, small change is *realistic*. It might be hard to find an hour to exercise, but it's easy to find a minute to do one jumping jack.

Second, small change is *fast*. Instead of trying to find a new career, you might do what my client Frankie did and call a colleague to arrange a lunch meeting. Instead of starting your massage business next week, you might do what my client Ellen did and offer one half-price massage to a friend. Once you take these small steps, you'll find it much easier to continue with your plan.

Third, small changes are *flexible*. They're small enough to fit a variety of situations. For example, Cory could take a few moments to relax before he got out of bed, before breakfast, after he got in his car, or even during a staff meeting. Although a longer practice is helpful, these more flexible versions of breath work are invaluable.

Fourth, small actions are *effective*, in that they increase the likelihood of success. You might forget to count calories; you're much more likely to remember to eat an apple before lunch or drink a glass of water before dinner. You might not write your entire business plan by Friday, but you can probably write one mediocre sentence on Tuesday morning.

Fifth, small change is *easier*. Let's consider, for example, one of Alexi's goals: "I'm going to make 40 phone calls to clients every workday, starting today." It's a worthy goal, and if Alexi can jump in and do it, great! But if she finds herself procrastinating, she can make it smaller. She could shrink this to "I'm going to call Jim Smith this afternoon at 2:30 pm." *That* feels much simpler.

In Chapter 7 ("Shrink"), you'll learn how to shrink your actions until they're doable, flexible, and successful. This process will help you create forward movement right away.

Act

Consistent action is the next step in the process of change. You've already come up with actions that are connected to your values, part of a thoughtful plan, and small enough to be successful. Now it's time to start moving by doing them regularly and consistently.

Through consistent, focused action, you'll be able to tell early on what's working and what's not. You'll learn what's possible for you and what you need to adjust. You'll also find out more about what you enjoy and how others will respond to what you do. If you like the results, simply continue. Your actions will turn into routines and habits and in that way become part of your life.

Consistent action is also the key to motivation – the desire or willingness to do something that matters. Habits keep you moving forward even when you don't feel inspired. Cory's goal, to stop worrying, was vague. However, he was able to take the consistent action of paying attention to his thoughts for just a few minutes a day. Karen's goal, to "find a new medical reception job by October," was overwhelming. So she updated the second paragraph of her resume, and then the third, and so forth until she was finished. For both of them, the actions became part of their routine.

Once your actions become automatic, you'll find yourself looking forward to them – or at least feel more willing to carry them out.

Action not only moves you forward, but it also changes your thoughts, feelings, and perception of yourself. Simply *doing something new* improves mental flexibility, creativity, the ability to respond to new things with ease, and the ability to look at a situation from different points of view.

There's also another part of action to consider – the role of your environment. A supportive environment helps make the action easy. When Laura (from Chapter 2) wanted to write, for example, she had paper, pens, and her laptop ready to go at her desk each morning. When my client David decided to go to the gym every morning, he left his workout clothes out on a chair and car keys in a pile on his dresser.

Chapter 8 ("Act") shows how small, thoughtful actions and a supportive environment can make change simple and automatic. Ultimately, neither willpower nor motivation is the driving force behind these changes. Rather, there is a predictable process: act, evaluate, and adjust, until the routines and habits you want are a part of your life. In Chapter 8, you'll learn how to do that.

Flow

Flow, in your life, is the ability to move past the inevitable obstacles in your path. No matter how good your plans, they'll need to be adjusted. You might need help that doesn't come through, run into a tough competitor, inadvertently upset a client, or miss an important meeting. Or the cause might be entirely outside of you – a promising investment doesn't pay off, your job disappears, or your house gets flooded.

It may sound obvious to say that life is full of obstacles, but much of the time we seem to think it shouldn't be. "Why is this so hard?" we wonder. We think of obstacles as something in the way, keeping us from the life we imagine. But when you climb a mountain, you expect it will be steep. In fact, that's exactly why we climb – for the challenge, or at least for the benefit of getting physically and mentally stronger.

The key to *flow,* to getting through tough times, is the ability to see failure as progress. Although there are real, external obstacles in life, the difficulty for most of us is getting past the internal ones – our *interpretation* of events and what they mean about *us*.

To *flow*, you'll need the ability to challenge your thoughts, the desire to change the stories you tell yourself, and the confidence to continue to take one micro-step after another in the direction of your goal. Your path will meander. You'll need to adjust frequently, thoughtfully, and sometimes quickly. Sometimes you'll need to change course entirely. But each of these adjustments is a chance to gain a new skill or learn something about yourself.

Flow is the process of moving around, over, under, or through obstacles. It's learning how to avoid them in the first place, when it's possible, and how to get back on your path when it's not. It's about recognizing the rare occasion when an obstacle truly signals a major change in course. Chapter 9 ("Flow") outlines six strategies you can use to stay in *flow*.

Celebrate

Celebration, quite simply, can change your life. It can help you stick with your goals and accomplish great things. Celebrations create momentum and enhance performance.[3]

There's more to celebration though. It also helps you notice progress. This helps resist a common human tendency to see what's wrong instead of what's right. It bypasses willpower by focusing on what's working instead of what you want to resist. If you unpacked one box or wrote one sentence, you've accomplished something. According to researcher Barbara L. Fredrickson, people who noticed that they were making significant behavioral change were 4.7 times more likely to maintain their new behavior 15 months later.[4] Why not acknowledge each step along the way?

Celebrations don't have to be large or elaborate. Rather, they are most inspiring and effective when they are small and happen often. One of the ways Anna (from Chapter 2) lost weight was by celebrating her walks. Instead of thinking of them as something she should do, Anna celebrated her two-mile circuit with an encouraging comment to herself.

Small celebrations take less than a minute, but help acknowledge the progress you're making. Internal dialog often changes from criticism to appreciation. With practice, you'll look forward to your tiny celebrations, and they will become part of what inspires you to move forward.

Four Truths about Change

Since you're working on making changes in your life, there are four basic truths you should know.

1. **You have to understand habits to create effective change.** Much of what we do every day consists of habits. Some of them are helpful and others not so much. Creating a positive new habit often means changing a not-so-helpful habit. If you

understand how habits work and how they are related to each other, you can find the point of greatest leverage to begin to make a change.

2. **Starting a new habit (or stopping a bad one) takes attention and persistence.** The change itself might take less than a minute, but during that minute you'll need to engage your frontal cortex and focus completely on the new habit. Popular thinking suggests that you'll need this new focus for 21 days, eight weeks, 90 days, or some other number of trials. The truth is, there's no magic number. Some habits are easier to create than others, and they might become automatic right away. Others are more challenging, and they might need your active focus for many months. If you assume your new, positive habit is automatic before it really is, you're likely to slide back onto the well-worn path of your old ways.

3. **Change is affected by people and circumstances beyond your control.** This isn't a problem. It's just part of how life works. Most of the time, the strategies presented in this book will help you find your way around those circumstances so you can make the changes you want.

4. **Change might not look like you expected it to look.** For example, you might not get hired for a particular job, but with the right kind of effort you're likely to find a job that's a good fit for your skills.

The Power of Habits

Habits are simple, learned behaviors that guide what we do. Some are based on choice and intention, like taking an evening walk. Others are accidental, such as eating more food just because it's on your plate. Remarkably, the habits themselves are made up of even tinier processes that take place far below the level of our awareness, at the level of neurons.

Learning a new task means neurons that don't normally communicate begin to do so. Certain combinations of neural firing become more common and more automatic. New pathways are created in the brain. Each time you do something new, you create new connections between neurons. If you continue to act in a new desired way, the neural pathways are reinforced. So as you stick with a new behavior, your brain begins to support it more and more. If you go back to the old way, the newer pathways will start to fade.

Imagine water from a snowmelt trickling down the side of a mountain. Over time, the water carves a particular set of channels as it flows down the mountainside. If many trickles combine to form a stream or a river, the process is reinforced, and the effect is even more powerful.

As author John Arden argues, "You cannot change how you think and feel without changing your brain."[5] His thinking is in line with new ideas about neuroplasticity, a term that refers to that very ability.

One interesting study used functional MRIs to measure the effect of learning on the hippocampus of taxi drivers in London. These drivers navigate some 25,000 streets and thousands of specific London locations, then pass an exam to demonstrate their expertise. Researchers Katherine Woollett, Hugo Spiers, and Eleanor Maguire found that the complex learning involved has an effect on the taxi drivers' brains. The study compared them with bus drivers, who needed to learn only set routes, but who were matched to the taxi drivers in terms of overall driving experience. The amount of gray matter in the hippocampus for the taxi drivers (a part of the brain related to learning) was significantly larger than it was for a control group of bus drivers.[6] Another MRI study led by Joenna Driemeyer found that learning a complex activity (in this case learning to juggle) can change the brain's structure in just 7 days.[7]

Learning changes the brain by affecting the number and efficiency of the connections between your brain's neurons. Here's something else. When you start something new, your prefrontal cortex is active. This is the part of your brain that helps you plan, organize, and make decisions. It's also the part of your brain that gets you to do something you decide to do, even though you're worried or not in the mood.

As a habit becomes automatic, another part of the brain becomes more active – the basal ganglia. This is the part of the brain where automatic actions take place, such as motor activity and procedural memory (the type of memory that lets you play the piano, ride a bike, or type a letter even after years of non-practice).

The habits involved in these processes can consist of either behaviors, like getting off the freeway on Main Street after work, or patterns of thinking, like worry.

Habits of thought are particularly powerful. Neuropsychologist Rick Hanson argues that changing your "flow of thoughts" can help create new feelings, new ways of interacting with others, and new ways of being in the world. As a result, you become more adaptable and more resilient. It's easier to weather changes that happen around you.[8]

When you first change a habit, there's a pull back toward the original behavior. For example, when you finally find a way to free your evenings to spend with family, a crisis at work will send you back to your old habit of working at home. When you finally start jogging every day, a bout of the flu will send you back to the couch – even after you've recovered. When you understand how the brain works, it's easier to recognize and resist this pull. This in turn helps reinforce your new habit.

Understanding how the brain works also helps you interpret stressful events in context. Instead of resigning yourself to a life of working in the evenings or tossing in the exercise towel, you'll realize that falling back into old habits is a natural part of change, and you'll have a plan to help yourself get back on track.

Exercise 3.1

a. *Which of the steps to change are already easy for you? Which do you need to learn more about?*

b. *What habits do you have that give you energy, focus, and joy?*

c. *What habits make it hard for you to reach your goals?*

d. *Which habit would you most like to change?*

e. *If you knew that you could change any behavior, what would you be able to accomplish?*

Chapter 3 walked you through the essence of how to use simple actions to not only meet short-term goals, but also to make significant life changes. Next, Chapters 4 through 10 will show you the "how" of change by providing a deeper look at the seven steps introduced in this chapter. The book's final section will summarize what you've learned, and suggest how you might apply it to your life.

There are many suggestions presented in this book on how to create successful change. There is no single reliable path to change, and no single suggestion works for everyone. Choose the ideas and suggestions that work best for you, or use the examples as inspiration for creating new possibilities for yourself. If you choose *something* and take action, you'll be well on your way to creating the life you want.

The *Small Change, Big Results* Pre-Test

Which of the following statements are true for you at this time? Write them on your designated notepad or check them off in the *Small Change, Big Results Workbook*. Your answers will show you where you need to focus to make your proposed changes stick. There are a total of 31 items on the list.

Pause

+ I build personal time into each week.
+ I spend quality time with my family and friends.
+ I leave my work at work.
+ I get enough sleep.
+ I get enough exercise.
+ I plan time each week for rest and renewal, in the form of mindfulness, inspirational reading, meditation, yoga, walks in nature, a spiritual practice, or another method of my choosing.

Imagine

+ I understand the role of imagination in creating change.
+ I'm clear about my top four or five values.
+ Based on those values, I am able to create a vision that feels powerful and inspiring.
+ I've given my vision form (a written page, poster, or other reminder), so I can refer to it often.

Plan

+ I've selected one part of my vision to be my first goal.
+ I know the major steps I need to take in order to reach my goal.

- ✦ I know how to break down those steps into smaller steps so I can clearly see when I'm making progress.

- ✦ I understand how to use target dates to help myself stay on track with my goals.

- ✦ I take time each day to plan, so that I schedule plenty of time for each task I need to complete.

Shrink

- ✦ I understand the value of making small change.

- ✦ I know how to shrink my actions until they feel simple and easy.

- ✦ When I feel resistance, I make the task even easier.

Act

- ✦ I know how to create routines so that follow-through on my commitments becomes automatic.

- ✦ I know how to create an environment that makes taking action easy.

- ✦ I'm willing to ask for help when I need it.

Flow

- ✦ I'm comfortable with challenges; I see them as opportunities to stretch myself.

- ✦ I understand that failure is a possible path to making significant accomplishments.

- ✦ I'm willing to talk with people I trust about mistakes and wrong guesses, because I know that this moves me more quickly toward success.

- ✦ I understand the power of stories, and I use them to inspire myself.

+ I know how to change negative, self-sabotaging thoughts into thoughts that are truthful but encouraging.

+ I nurture my own creativity so I can find unusual solutions to important problems.

Celebrate

+ I regularly celebrate my success.

+ I understand the power of gratitude in creating change.

+ I build time into my day and week for rest and renewal.

+ I use small rewards to help myself keep moving forward.

Simple Actions That Help Create New Neural Networks

Now that you've finished the pre-test, it's time to start the process of taking simple actions to create change. If you'd like to build new neural networks by doing something novel just for the fun of it, there are some suggestions below.

+ Drive home using a different route.

+ Learn something new: how to greet someone in Turkish, one new chord on the guitar, the basic rules of the game *Go!*

+ Read something new. If you like novels, try science. If you usually enjoy history, read a mystery.

+ Sleep on the other side of the bed.

+ Change your morning or evening routine.

+ Step outside your home or place of work. Look for something that's been there all along which you've never really noticed.

+ Write with your left hand for five minutes a day for a few weeks.

+ If you're introverted, try introducing yourself to someone new. If you're extroverted, experiment with a quiet evening at home.

Part II:

The Steps

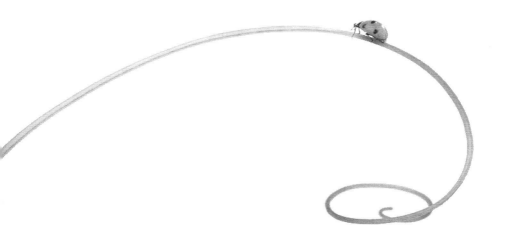

Chapter 4

Pause

*"Human freedom involves our capacity to pause between
the stimulus and response and, in that pause, to choose the one
response toward which we wish to throw our weight."*

– Rollo May, *The Courage to Create*

Quiet moments taken between tasks and projects are powerful. Such pauses are like the white space around the print on a page, the silence before the orchestra starts, the ocean surrounding an island. They put a spotlight on the work you do and give it meaning.

A pause is simply a way to relax, to gain perspective, and to reduce the effects of stress. Stress comes from thoughts about the future, and an effective antidote is to bring one's attention to the present moment. Most people would agree that learning to reduce stress is a good idea. Research on stress-reduction dates back to the 1950s.[1]

For many reasons, though, *pausing* is hard to put into practice. For some people, their *busyness* has momentum and it's hard to stop. Some people aren't sure where to find time for a break, and some don't feel they deserve one. For others, pausing allows uncomfortable feelings to surface – boredom, worry, or sadness – while staying in motion helps keep these feelings at bay.

In the end, though, by taking a few minutes to notice what you're thinking and feeling, you'll feel refreshed and re-energized. These small breaks interrupt the constant flow of thought and action, of planning and busyness, in a way that makes you more productive. Pausing takes you out of operating on automatic, enables you to be more aware of how you really think and feel, and allows difficult feelings to ease. Ultimately, by pausing, you'll have more choices.

The Power of Thought

One reason pausing is so important is that it can increase your awareness of how you're thinking. Why is this so crucial? Let's try a little experiment that will demonstrate how much your thinking can affect you. Read the following paragraph while paying attention to what is going on in your body.

Imagine that you're holding a fresh, crisp red apple. As you bite into it, you savor its sweet, slightly tart mouth-watering flavor. The taste gets sweeter as you chew each bite slowly, enjoying the apple's firm crunchiness.

As you read the sentences above, what happened in your body? Could you imagine the familiar flavors of a perfect apple? Did your mouth start to water? If so, that's a natural response. Simply reading a description can start your body's digestive process by releasing enzymes. This apple is only a thought, but in just a few moments that thought has the power to affect your physiology. Remarkably, in certain circumstances, your brain can't tell the difference between thoughts and real-world experiences.

You might have had an emotional response as well. If you like apples, the thought might have brought to mind the simple pleasure of a bite of good food. If the last apple you had was mushy or bland, or if you don't like apples, perhaps your response was one of distaste.

Your thoughts affect both your *body's responses* and your *emotions*, and there's plenty of research behind this. For instance, the relationship between *thought* and *mood* has been studied at major universities and other research centers throughout the world. It is the basis of the highly effective psychotherapeutic approach called Cognitive Behavioral Therapy (CBT),[2] as well as the increasingly popular practice of *mindfulness*.

The relationship between thought and *physiology* has also been studied. Thoughts lead to the production of chemicals, which affect blood pressure, perspiration, muscle tension, and ease of breathing. What you're thinking can affect digestion, immune functioning, metabolism, and many other physiological processes.[3] Thoughts can also affect your health, the quality of your relationships, your ability to focus and handle pressure, and your general level of happiness.[4]

The good news is that by deliberately changing your thoughts, you can change your experience.

Under the Surface

Let's look a bit deeper at the importance of this first step, *pause*. As we noted, pausing gives you time to look beneath the surface, moving your attention from what you're doing or what you see around you to what's happening inside – *your thoughts and feelings.*

Most of what happens in your mind is out of your awareness. Your thought process is in a way like an iceberg – a tiny bit is above the water and visible, while the rest is submerged and out of sight. With icebergs, the invisible mass isn't a problem in the untraveled waters of the Arctic. However, if the iceberg floats into an area where ships travel, it can create a dangerous situation.

Likewise, the real danger in your thinking is the part you *can't see*. As human beings, we need a way to become more aware of our thoughts, and you can't see your thoughts if you are constantly moving.

Keep in mind that your brain is active all the time, taking care of important physiological processes. You don't need to think, *"I'm going to digest something, so I guess I'll salivate now."* Remember how a cascade of chemical reactions automatically took place in response to your imagined bite of the apple?

You have a similar experience when you have thoughts like "*I'm going to be late*" or "*I have to go faster.*" This type of thought can lead to the heightened physiological activity of stress and the habit of staying busy. As you read in Chapter 2, staying "crazy busy" is among the major reasons that people fail at making positive changes in their lives.

Here's the key: If you can change your thoughts, you can change how you feel, how you think, and how you respond.

Alexi's Overloaded "To Do" List

Remember Alexi, the financial advisor from Chapter 1 who was working long hours and not making enough income? She wanted to spend more time with friends, take walks in the evenings, or curl up on weekends with a novel. She couldn't do any of this while she was constantly busy.

But her "to do" list was enormous, and her life was a blur. "It's just until I catch up," she assured me. "Besides, how can I take time out when I'm already so far behind?"

It wasn't a matter of time, but a matter of prioritizing her well-being. Alexi needed time to reflect on her goals, savor her accomplishments, and focus on the things that truly made a difference for her business. The time she chose was at the beginning of her workday.

Her new routine was to spend 10 minutes each morning in her yard, simply enjoying the natural world around her. When she arrived at work half an hour later, she made a cup of tea, sat down with her calendar, and took another ten minutes to plan her day. This simple routine was the beginning of a bigger change in Alex's mindset, and the beginning of a new way of thinking about her work. We'll see more of her in Chapter 5, "Imagine."

Simple Practices that Increase Well-Being

Pausing isn't always easy, as you know if you've tried to relax or meditate or change your thoughts. However, there are many ways to learn to pause, and the benefits are well worth it. There are two keys to making this work:

1. You need to consciously choose to spend the time.

2. You need to make this a regular part of your routine.

When you can do these two things, then you'll be able to integrate quiet time into your life.

The evidence-based practices below can be adapted to the amount of time you have, from 30 seconds to a daily 30- to 60-minute practice. I've helped students adapt these to use during a stressful exam and professionals to use them just before a presentation. When integrated into a daily routine, they bring more presence, focus, and calm to every activity. At the end of the chapter, there is a list of additional, less formal ways to pause.

The Relaxation Response

Harvard physician Herbert Benson was one of the first medical doctors in the U.S. to study the effects of relaxation on the mind and body. Originally Benson studied the effects of Transcendental Meditation (TM) on the body, and he found that people who practiced it, over time, were able to significantly reduce their blood pressure and heart rate, as well as slow their breathing. The results of his research were first published in 1975 as the book *The Relaxation Response.*[5] The Relaxation Response is also the term Benson coined for the body's ability to slow down under certain conditions.

As a doctor, Benson was interested in the stress-reducing effects of meditation. He understood that some 60% of visits to doctors' offices are stress-related or stress-induced. Stress can cause headaches, back pain, high blood pressure, asthma, insomnia, anxiety, and a variety of other conditions.

The Relaxation Response provides an antidote by calming the mind to relax the body. The idea that the mind can affect the body is a concept that has been supported by extensive research. Even a few minutes of focus each day can help enhance the immune system.[6] The method doesn't depend on any particular kind of meditation or belief system. Even focused breathing can help bring relaxation and awareness.

Kristin, one of my clients, used her breath to stay calm through the course of her cancer treatment. First, she tried 30 minutes of meditation twice a day. Although it took the edge off her anxiety, it didn't bring forth the calmer state of mind she was hoping for. We decided to increase the frequency, so that she spent 5 minutes every hour doing a relaxed breathing exercise – enough time for about 60 breaths. Remembering to do this every hour was a challenge, so she set her phone to signal discreetly as her "breathing time" approached, and to act as a reminder to pause and breathe.

After a few weeks, Kristin felt noticeably calmer. When she finally finished a lengthy and difficult chemotherapy, Kristin said that these small moments of breathing were what helped her through it. Five minutes every hour meant that she had about an hour a day to re-orient, stop her mind from spinning, and relax.

If a few minutes of breathing every hour can help someone in this kind of crisis, imagine what it could do to ease ordinary moments of indecision, worry, and stress.

There are many other methods of working with the breath. In The Healing Power of the Breath, psychiatrists describe several methods of breathing that have been shown to reduce stress, improve performance, and promote calm and healing.[7] One of the more popular relaxation practices that can incorporate attention to the breath is mindfulness.

Mindfulness

Mindfulness is essentially the art of paying attention. Its roots are originally in Buddhism. A popular and secular version of mindfulness, Mindfulness-Based Stress Reduction (MBSR) was introduced in 1979 by Jon Kabbat-Zinn, Ph.D., at the University of Massachusetts Medical School. At first, he taught mindfulness as a way to reduce chronic pain. Since then, it has developed into a well-researched and nationally known practice that helps people change the way they respond to the stressful events of life. The practice of MBSR is outlined in Kabbat-Zinn's book, *Full Catastrophe Living.*[8]

Mindfulness can be practiced in many ways. One way is to meditate by sitting comfortably and focusing on your breath. As you sit, notice the rise and fall of your abdomen as you inhale and exhale. When your mind wanders, as it inevitably will, just bring your attention gently back to your breath. Kristin used a version of this practice when she paused every hour. Instead of always sitting, though, she used those moments to pay attention while walking or standing.

We take about 16 breaths a minute when we're relaxed, which comes to about 16,300 breaths during the 17-odd hours we're awake each day. If you can learn to pay attention to just a few of your breaths, every day, you'll end up feeling calmer, healthier, and surprisingly more productive.

Mindfulness creates a kind of re-focusing that helps you let go of the past and future and live in the present moment. Instead of thinking about what you did last week, what you should be doing right now, and what you might do tomorrow, your attention is simply on your breath. The more you practice, the better you get at being present. Since stress is largely about the future, mindfulness helps reduce feelings of stress.

You may recall that Cory, the software engineer, had a habit of worrying about things that might happen in the future. As he learned to be more mindful, he started to observe his worried thoughts instead of getting caught up in them. When a worry came up, he simply noticed it. "Oh, there's that worry again," he told himself. When thoughts are noticed but not engaged with, they tend to lose energy. For Cory, over time, worry eased.

As mindfulness deepens with practice, you can for a time become immersed in the present. When this happens, there are no worries – no thoughts about the past or future, no fears, no fantasies – just whatever is happening at the moment. It's a little like being "in the zone" while playing a sport. You're aware of everything at once – your teammates, the ball, the referees. It's as if you're caught in a slow-motion replay, and you have all the time you need to make the right choice. There are no distractions, and you know exactly what you need to do.

You don't need to be an athlete to experience this sense of flow. Anytime you are completely immersed in what you are doing, aware of your surroundings but not distracted by them, moving from one step to another with ease, you are there. That kind of presence can be cultivated with mindfulness, as long as you make time for it and incorporate it into your daily routine.

Moments of mindful pausing add up over time to bring more benefits. One study found measurable changes in the brain after just 8 weeks of daily meditation.[9] In another, researchers noted that after subjects experienced 11 hours of meditation over 4 weeks, there were changes in their brains' white matter, a pale tissue that helps different parts of the brain communicate.

Please note: If you are new to meditation, the best way to start is to take a Mindfulness-Based Stress Reduction class or to seek out an experienced meditation teacher. Sometimes, during meditation, emotions and memories can bubble up, and a teacher can show you how to handle those things. However, whether or not you meditate, you can learn to be more mindful in any area of your life.

A Simple Mindfulness Practice

1. Sit comfortably.

2. Set a pleasant-sounding timer for 5 to 10 minutes.

3. Bring your attention to your breath.

4. Your mind will inevitably wander. You'll experience thoughts, feelings, and physical sensations. When you notice this, bring your attention back to your breath in a quiet, nonjudgmental way. Don't worry about how many times this happens – just notice.

5. When you hear the timer, take a deep breath, and then move to your next activity.

Creating Pauses in Relationships

In relationships, pause takes the form of spending positive time with someone you care about. This means time when you're not making dinner, paying bills, supervising homework, or responding to texts. Rather, it's time when you can sit together and talk, or head out for a walk or movie.

A few years ago, I asked one of the couples I was working with, Donna and Eli, how they planned to stay connected with each other while working toward career goals and raising kids. Donna said, "We don't have enough time to do things with just each other. We're hoping that our relationship is strong enough to keep us connected until our daughter is grown."

They wanted to put their relationship on hold for about eight years, banking on the goodwill they felt in the early days. But already there was strain. Although they smiled and joked, there were also misunderstandings that weren't getting resolved. They had time for work, family, cooking, chores, parenting, and friends – *but not each other.*

The things we value most in relationships – love, safety, romance, affection, desire – don't easily fit on a "to-do" list. Time is part of the rich soil that sustains relationships. Pausing – making room for relaxed, unscheduled time – allows for new conversations and new ways of being together.

Digging Deeper

If pausing feels difficult, it might not be about schedules or about packing too much into busy lives. Sometimes difficulty finding time is about *emotion*. Couples often tell me early on that it's impossible to find relationship time. What I repeatedly hear underneath their words is that it's *uncomfortable* to spend unstructured time together.

My clients Sandra and Jay found themselves in this situation. They were facing many pressures – including a shared business that didn't quite make ends meet, and a blended family.

Time was indeed scarce, and both Sandra and Jay were exhausted by the end of the day. They disagreed about how chores should be shared and about how weekend time should be divided. They'd tried talking it out, but the tension was high, so they often "solved" problems by ignoring them.

The "ignore it" solution makes sense in a way. Most of us prefer to tackle problems we can solve rather than ones we don't understand. It's hard to talk about what's simmering under the surface in a relationship. It's hard to bring up disappointments and difficult moments without sounding critical. It's hard to talk about deep longings and needs in a relationship when you're not really clear about how you feel, or when you're afraid your partner won't understand.

But when couples can't talk about disappointments and longings, a kind of tension develops, and they start to avoid spending time together. It can happen almost automatically. That part of the brain that tries to keep us safe starts to focus on what feels manageable – work, friends, the

3 Ways to Pause in a Relationship

1. **Start small:** If you can't find an hour a week, start with 10 minutes. If a night out isn't in your budget, walk around the neighborhood together. One couple had a "date" every Friday night at home. Their kids ate early, helped re-set the table, then disappeared into their rooms for an hour. Then the couple had dinner alone together. These Friday nights became an enjoyable time for the whole family.

2. **Develop rituals:** Create something that happens almost automatically. One couple has dinner out every Tuesday. Another couple takes a long walk every Friday afternoon. Some of my clients have coffee or lunch together after a counseling session.

3. **Plan ahead:** Schedule something in advance that is hard to change. One couple bought season tickets to a community theater. Their "dates" went into their calendars months in advance, and they looked forward to each evening together. Another couple arranged a child care swap with another family for a set time every two weeks.

"to do" list. The intention is good, but the result is problematic – couples start to drift apart.

One benefit of couples counseling is that it provides time for new, more collaborative conversations. Over time, the conversations that start in sessions spill over into daily life. Relationship-time allows each partner to begin to see the other differently.

Sandra and Jay started with relaxed time together every day, which evolved into a regular Saturday hike. They built into their day both positive time for appreciation and planning time for their business. Coming together in this way at the beginning and end of their workday was key in sorting through their differences and building closeness. As Sandra and Jay were more able to *pause* to talk about their hopes and dreams, the relationship started to blossom again.

Exercises

Write your response to the following exercises in a notebook or in the *Small Change, Big Results Workbook.*

Exercise 4.1

· ·

Where in your life could you use a pause?

· ·

Exercise 4.2

· ·

Most people find it hard to pause. The pace of life is so fast and there is so much to be done. What are some of the things that make it hard for you to pause?

· ·

Exercise 4.3

· ·

There is no single right way to pause. You might already have a regular practice that allows you to relax and renew. If not, several ways have been presented in this chapter, and there are many others. Choose one to try this week.

· ·

Where Can You Find 5 Minutes?

The minutes you need are everywhere around you. They're in every conversation, every activity, every step of your day. On the next page are some possibilities:

- **The beginning or end of every day.** Take a few minutes to reflect on your day to make sure the activities you have planned are aligned with your energy and skills. Also, think about what you truly believe is important. When you have too many tasks and not enough time, it's like cramming too many things into an overstuffed closet. There's not room for all of it, so some things fall on the floor. Tasks get dropped. Appointments get forgotten, perhaps double-booked, or not booked at all. When you're on automatic pilot, you're not choosing what gets dropped. A pause can help you look at the big picture and make choices that reflect your values.

- **The end of a task.** The way you start something has a lot to do with how it turns out. A few minutes of thought at the start of a project can help you move in the right direction and save wasted effort. A few moments, a few breaths, or a simple cup of tea between tasks can help clear your mind, so you can bring a fresh focus to the task you're doing next.

- **During a heated discussion.** A pause can stop an argument in its tracks. Instead of responding out of anger or frustration, take a few breaths to consider what you really want to say and how you want to say it. Is what you're about to say the best way to get your partner on board? Will your wording sound respectful to your colleague?

- **Anytime.** To pause is to be present. It's the opposite of being swept along by the tide of events. It's being able to look, however briefly, at all of the possible paths in front of you, and choose the one that is the most interesting, compelling, or fun.

Taking time to reflect helps you get clear about what is right for you now and in this situation. It's about taking a moment, a day, or a week if needed, to consider what you want to hold on to and what to let go of.

Exercise 4.4

When in your day can you find 5 minutes? Write your answers in a notebook, or use the checklist in the Small Change, Big Result Workbook.

You might choose a particular time...

+ Before you get up
+ As soon as you get up
+ Right after breakfast
+ Right after lunch
+ After you brush your teeth
+ Just before bedtime
+ Just before you close your eyes

Or you might choose to link your 5 minutes to an event...

+ After your partner leaves for work
+ The moment you step into the shower
+ After the kids leave for school
+ After you pick up your keys to leave in the morning
+ Before you start your car
+ Between phone calls
+ When you finish a task and before you start a new one
+ During a tense discussion
+ At the end of the meeting

Exercise 4.5

Mark that time in your calendar for the next week. Check every day that you are able to practice. What's it like to pause for 5 minutes? How do you feel? What changes do you notice?

There are thousands of opportunities to pause every day. It takes just moments to notice your breathing, to reflect on your day, to silently repeat a word or phrase, to consider what you're about to say, or to check in with your body. Choose one... or more. Over time, this will transform your health and your life.

Pause is a part of a natural cycle of work and play, activity and rest. We'll revisit the idea in Chapter 6 ("Plan"), with the discussion of downtime, and again in Chapter 10 ("Celebrate"), when we look at the importance of celebrating. Imagining, the subject of the next chapter, is also a type of pause. By taking time out to imagine what you find most inspiring, you build energy that helps move you toward your goal. Chapter 5 demonstrates how to do this.

And while you're at it, enjoy a bite of a crisp, fresh apple.

Key Points

+ By changing your thoughts, you can change your experience.

+ A pause helps slow down the rush of activity so you can better see what really matters.

+ Taking time to bring about the "relaxation response" through breathing or practicing mindfulness has huge benefits. For example, it can reduce stress, improve mood, increase well-being, and enhance your immune system.

+ Even a small amount of meditation practice creates visible changes in your brain, and can result in more relaxation and ease.

Simple Actions to Help You Pause

There are many ways to practice Pause in your daily life. You can choose something specific to help you through a difficult situation or a more general practice to support well-being. Several possibilities are described below.

+ **Shrug.** Raise your shoulders to your ears, and notice the feeling of tension that winds into your abdomen, chest, and neck. Then let your shoulders drop down, arms hanging from your shoulder girdle. Notice how much of the tension disappears. Savor the feeling of relaxation that replaces it.

+ **Give yourself a massage.** A massage can be relaxing and restful. Give yourself a mini-massage by using your right hand to massage your left. Search for the areas where the massaging works best, that give you the most sense of release. After about a minute, switch hands.

+ **Have a cup of tea.** Enjoy a cup of warm tea, hot cider, or hot chocolate. The warmth is soothing, and you might recall some pleasant memories associated with special treats, warm winter evenings, or campfires.

+ **Sip a glass of cold lemonade** in the shade if the weather is warm.

+ **Walk.** Step outside for a few minutes and breathe in the fresh air, or then take a short walk. Sometimes a few minutes of physical activity can "re-set" your brain and help you approach a problem from a different perspective.

+ **Laugh.** It's hard to feel anxious when you're laughing. Turn off the news for a while and read something funny. Listen to your favorite comedian, take in a comedy show, watch a "kitten video" on YouTube, or simply notice the funny moments that are part of everyday life. Even the act of smiling can create a positive shift in your mood.

+ **Listen to music.** Music can soothe anxiety. Bring your favorite songs to work, or listen to them while you're making dinner. For some people, a favorite piece of music can transport them to a time of relaxation and enjoyment. Experiment. Notice your level of calm before and after a piece of music, and find the music that works best for you.

+ **Give.** Research shows that we feel less busy if we give time away. It sounds backward, but a recent study from Harvard, Yale, and the University of Pennsylvania showed that doing something for others changes one's own subjective sense of time. Activities like writing a letter to a sick child or spending 30 minutes doing something for someone else left people feeling like they had more time than control groups who wasted time or spent it on themselves.[10]

+ **Do something fun.** Enjoy an ice cream cone, buy a balloon, climb a tree, try a hula hoop, blow bubbles, or doodle. Do something fun, just because you want to, and enjoy the emotional boost. Include at least a few minutes of fun in each day.

+ **Daydream.** Remember a joyful moment from the past. Perhaps there was a time when you did something well, or a moment when someone offered you much needed support. Maybe it was a smile or words of encouragement from someone close to you... or a complete stranger. Recall the memory and notice a sense of well-being.

Chapter 5

Imagine

"Logic will get you from A to Z;
imagination will get you everywhere."

– Albert Einstein

Imagining **your goal is** a powerful way to start moving toward it. For example, what kind of work feels so much in your nature that it would seem like play? What essential qualities in relationships would help support, nurture, and challenge you, all at once? What mission would inspire you day after day?

Once you have imagined your dream in exquisite detail, it will illuminate your path like the beacon from a lighthouse. It will be your compass in the wilderness. It will keep you on your path, even when all the "crazy busy" forces in the world conspire against you. It will help you navigate successfully through the hundreds of small distractions you encounter every day.

Imagining is about choosing a life that is meaningful to you and developing the inner resources to help you attain it. It's a creative process. To begin, consider the following questions. Write your answers on a notepad or in the *Small Change, Big Results Workbook* as you go along.

Exercise 5.1

* *Look back at the values you identified in the section "Your Heart Isn't in It" from Chapter 2. Those values are the footprint, or foundation, from which you build. It's hard to build a mansion on the footprint of a cottage or a seaside cabin on the footprint of a condominium. Fine-tune this list of values if you'd like.*

* *Now consider your talents and skills. When you look back over your life so far, what have you done well? Maybe it's organizing, or coaching, or negotiating deals, or entertaining kids, or nurturing sick animals. Maybe this is something you want to imagine as part of your future as well.*

* *What activities do you love doing? Do you enjoy helping people, building homes, making jewelry, or clearing trails? These interests are clues that can help point you toward the things that uniquely fit your passions and talents.*

* *What pastimes do you find yourself engaged in during the idle moments of your day? Maybe you drift toward designing clothes, or writing poetry, or solving puzzles.*

Once you have some answers, look through them to see if you can find a pattern. Let's say, for example, that you're contemplating a new line of work. Maybe your happiest moments are playing with dogs. Maybe you're especially good at handling canines, even the hard-to-manage ones. When you see a pattern like this, explore it further. Consider guiding questions like these:

* Do you not only like dogs, but also have an interest in medicine and healing?

* Do you also like dealing with pet owners in crisis?

* Are you good at helping people make difficult decisions about their pets?

If these are your skills, you might enjoy becoming a vet.

Maybe you prefer to be around healthy dogs and like driving around. If you'd also enjoy spending time wandering through parks with six dogs on a leash, you might consider creating your own business as a dog walker. If you don't care for driving and would rather people bring their pooches to you, perhaps having your own dog training or dog grooming business is more of a fit. If you don't want the responsibility of owning a business, maybe working at a "doggie day care" is worth a try?

Each time you consider a possible direction, ask yourself what parts of it match your skills and interests, and which parts would leave you inspired.

This isn't a one-time process. Over time, the things that inspire you will change. You continually gain new skills and test new interests. Each life transition is an opportunity to review your life and look for the things you're best at, most proud of, or most passionate about. It's from this vantage point that you can imagine a future worth pursuing. The best time to imagine the work, practices, and relationships that would make you happy for the rest of your life is always *now*.

The Science behind Imagining

Imagination is supremely practical. Hundreds of studies over the past 30 years have shown that imagining an outcome in exquisite detail helps performance, creativity, and healing.[1] Along with real-life practice, imagination enhances performance for musicians, actors, singers, basketball players, skiers, and tennis players. In many situations, the brain has a hard time distinguishing physical activity from mental, so the mental work of imagining bestows physical benefits.[2]

It's not just physical abilities that improve, though. Creating a clear, mental picture of what you want makes results more likely. The process isn't all that mysterious. First, a clear and detailed vision helps *define* the change you want. For instance, you'd be lucky to end up with a dream vacation if you just told your travel agent that you'd like to go "someplace nice." In the same way, you're unlikely to be satisfied if your goal is to simply "get fit." Do you want to develop more endurance, to acquire muscle strength, to recover from an injury, or to learn to ski? Imagining, in detail, helps you know *what* you want, and therefore it can also assist in determining a path toward it.

Second, imagining helps you *focus*. We have only so much energy, and not everything we encounter enters into our conscious awareness. What you notice and what you don't depends a lot on your mindset. Let's say you imagine yourself as a successful, published novelist. As you go about your day, you might hear a friend make a comment about writing, something that would have slipped by if "writing a novel" wasn't foremost in your mind. You might spot an inspiring story that connects to your theme, or notice a flier for a beginning novelist writers group – things that might have escaped your focus if you hadn't imagined your goal. In this way, imagining helps you find resources that would otherwise have remained unnoticed.

On the physical level, new patterns of thinking create new neural networks, and lead to the release of hormones like cortisol, which in turn boost your energy level and mood. With persistence, you can slowly but steadily become the person you want to be.

"Tweaking" or Transforming?

Imagining your goal can help with problems both large and small, and it can help you with any of these goals:

+ You want to make a relatively small change.
+ You have a big goal and you're not sure how to achieve it.
+ You want to reinvent yourself.

It's not always clear at the beginning which of these possibilities you'll choose. Let's look at each of them.

You want to make a small change. My client David wanted to get fit. He had the time and the knowledge, but wasn't able to get started. For inspiration, David imagined how he'd feel as he pushed past the finish line of a 10k race, how he'd look in a new pair of jeans, and the compliments he'd get from friends about his newfound energy. We'll see in Chapter 6 ("Plan") how he then used this vision to create a plan that kept him going.

You have a big goal and you're not sure how to achieve it. When Alexi realized that her business wasn't working, she had to ask herself some difficult questions. Was she in the right line of work? What was she passionate about?

A *successful* financial advisor spends hours a day on the phone, checking in with clients and contacting prospective investors. This was the one task Alexi was for the most part neglecting, and it was the heart of her business. She did answer calls as they came in, but she wasn't being proactive in making new calls, even though she had a long list of people who had expressed interest in the kind of services she offered. Alexi had become caught up in the myriad of distractions and interruptions of her day, without stepping back to understand why. As a result, she was missing out on a ton of new business.

It became clear in our conversations that Alexi needed to make about 40 calls a day, and she had been avoiding those calls. She had to ask herself why. Was it because she wasn't good at making them, or because she didn't like it? If so, the job she had might not be a good match for her, and she'd be better off finding something that fit her talents.

Since Alexi loved finance, maybe a behind-the-scenes job like accounting would be a better fit. She seemed to find plenty of time to mentor others, so perhaps teaching was more her calling. Before moving forward, we had to spend some time thinking through these possibilities.

Alexi decided to continue on the path she was on. Even though she had been procrastinating, Alexi enjoyed talking with new people. She liked to work with clients one-on-one to resolve their financial issues.

What Alexi needed next was a clear picture of the kind of life she wanted and tools to manage the many demands on her time. Before she bought a new time-management system and jumped in, however, she wisely took the time to imagine her ideal workday. She wanted more than anything a sense of ease, so her vision included not just the activities she would do, but how she would feel.

She envisioned an ideal workday where her only task for the first few uninterrupted hours was to check in with clients and potential clients. She imagined talking with each of her clients by phone every month and face-to-face twice a year. She would hire a top-notch administrative assistant to manage the scheduling and administrative tasks, so she could spend her time making connections and doing financial analyses. Her calls would be comfortably completed by mid-afternoon, and it was then that she would start the mentoring and collaborating that had been taking up much of her days. By then, she'd be feeling relaxed and energized. Alexi would be caught up on her projects, and she'd have a system for deciding when to say yes to new ones. She would then leave work by 6:00 pm to enjoy the rest of her evening at home or with friends.

Alex's vision was of a smoothly running workday and the ability to focus on the things that were most important. It addressed her particular challenges with focus and attention, and it also brought her joy. For you, a vision might be to find a new living situation, reclaim time with your family, find a way to work with a difficult colleague, or spend three months living in another country.

You want to reinvent yourself. Sandra, on the other hand, was having trouble in her marriage, with her stepchildren, and with her business. Sandra's share of the work was mostly administrative, and she performed it adequately. It didn't require her significant graphic design talents, and she missed the opportunity to use them. Sandra wanted work she enjoyed, a marriage that felt close and connected, and a family that could have fun on the weekends. Her vision included every part of her life. We'll take a look at part of Sandra's vision – more of the specifics of what she imagined for herself – later in this chapter.

Imagining on this larger scale is also helpful when you're young and first leaving home, and you don't know yet know what you want to do. It can also guide you when you have a career but it isn't what you expected it to be, or when a relationship is ending, your kids are leaving home, or you're about to retire and wondering what's next.

Exercise 5.2

1. Use your answers from Exercise 5.1 to choose what you'd like to change. Will it be:

+ A change in a small and very specific part of your life?

+ A big goal?

+ A major transformation?

2. Write a brief statement of your goal.

+ **Example 1.** David's goal: I'm going to run a 10k by the end of April.

+ **Example 2.** Alexi's goal: I want to build my business and create a sense of ease in my day.

+ **Example 3.** If you, like Sandra, are looking for a major transformation, choose for now one aspect of it. Sandra chose this: I want a warm and loving relationship with Jay, in which we enjoy each other's company and find time for each other every day.

Now write yours.

From Goals to Vision

I first learned about the power of imagining and the process of creating a vision from Katherine. She was head of a very successful real estate team, and I was fortunate to be able to attend a retreat she facilitated for her staff some 30 years ago. These retreats were part of how she brought her vision to life, and she went through the process every year with her staff. During the retreat, Katherine shared how she had used imagining to help make her career change into real estate.

Katherine had worked as a social worker for 15 years, and she wanted to reinvent herself. There were things about her former job she loved: the contact with people; the need for good organizational skills; and the ability to help people in crisis make decisions and follow through. These were things she wanted to bring into her new line of work in real estate.

She wanted to add some new things as well. Katherine wanted to give up her 45 minute commute and work in her community. She also wanted the leadership opportunity of designing and running her own business. After brainstorming dozens of possibilities, talking with friends, and doing some serious soul-searching, Katherine set a goal: she decided to become a residential real estate broker and create a successful real estate agency.

Once Katherine got her broker's license, she bought into a well-known franchise. However, the reality she first encountered was far different from what she had expected. "There were two burned out agents and a secretary," Katherine said. "Sales were rare, and incoming calls were few. The agent weren't productive. But more importantly, they weren't happy. Their goal seemed to be simply to get through the day."

Katherine knew then that she had a choice. "I could become part of that low-energy, going-through-the-motions culture, or I could change it. I knew the change would take years, and that it would be difficult, but taking on that challenge meant everything to me. So I started with a vision."

Katherine's vision was written in the present tense so it felt more immediate and tangible. It sounded something like this:

> Our office is beautiful – freshly painted and spotlessly clean. But my favorite part of being a broker is working with my five sales associates, each of whom is a licensed real estate agent. They come to the office each day energized and ready to work. Each of them sets personal goals that are challenging, and each year they surprise themselves with what they accomplish. Because I've spent so many years working with people, I can spot problems while they're still minor, and I help people learn to work through them and learn to support each other. Our staff training is known as the best in the business, and because of that, many agents apply to work with us. I'm able to hire staff members who are committed to their work and also willing to collaborate and cooperate with others in the office.

Her vision included the people she would hire, their level of enthusiasm, the training they would need, and the systems that would support them. She imagined their connections in the community, their relationships with each other, and their income. Katherine posted her vision where she'd see it every day. Every decision she made, every action she took, was based on that vision. It affected her hiring, as well as how she went about developing what became known as one of the best new-agent training programs in the area.

Slowly but surely the office culture changed. One of the original associates felt energized by Katherine's new way of thinking and eventually became a top producer; the other associate left. New hires were made based on a commitment to personal goals as well as an ability to collaborate. Over a decade, Katherine built one of the most successful real estate agencies in her area. With her success came the lifestyle she wanted, including month-long vacations with her family during the low season each December.

Katherine taught her staff this method of creating a vision, and over the years, I've used it myself and with others I have supervised. I've refined the process to help my staff, my students, and clients become clearer about their deepest desires and what it would take to accomplish them.

Exercise 5.3

· ·

Take the goal you developed in Exercise 5.2, and rewrite it as a vision of your ideal project, day, job, or relationship. Spend some time with this. It's worth it.

· ·

Embellishing Your Vision

One of the major reasons people give up on change is because *they can't see it happening.* People often dismiss real progress and throw in the towel. *Detail* is a way to bring your compelling goal into focus, so you know exactly what you're aiming for. It also enables you to recognize that you are indeed moving forward with your vision.

To explore the concept, try to imagine this one-sentence novel: "Someone has to bring a valuable object to a dangerous place." Because it's not specific, this tiny "'novel'" is not inspiring. However, when approximately 450,000 words of detail were added, J.R.R. Tolkien came up with the captivating fantasy *Lord of the Rings.*[3]

Adding detail accomplishes several things:

1. **It's a way of testing your dream by giving it form.** You really can't be sure that a goal is worth the effort until you can picture it. "I want my own business" sounds lovely until you imagine yourself providing a service, plus doing the marketing, keeping up with the financial records, making the phone calls,

and the dozens of other tasks that you need to take care of every week. When you add detail, it's easier to see whether your vision calls for an excited "Yes!" or a more thoughtful "Never mind."

2. **The more detailed you are, the more likely that your vision will take physical form.** If you're looking for treasure but you don't know exactly where it is, it's easy to wander down side alleys or miss a critical turn that would speed you on your way. When you know your destination, you can take the straightest path there, and avoid obstacles that could cost valuable time and energy.

3. **It's the details that make your vision personal.** A hundred people might want to learn to act, but the details will point each person toward his or her dream. One person might want to join a community theater, another to appear on a New York City stage, and a third to make it in Hollywood. More detail makes it even more personal. Some people who are passionate about community theater prefer improvisation, while others lean toward Shakespeare. One person might want the lead role, while another prefers to sing in the chorus.

Let's look at how Alexi, Cory, and Sandra added detail to their goals.

Alexi imagined arriving at work early, spending the morning comfortably and easily making her needed calls, and managing the rest of her tasks in the afternoon. She wrote about finishing projects and supervising. She also did some research on the cost of retirement, figured out how much she would need to save, and put those numbers into her vision. Alexi's language looked something like this:

> I start my calls by 8:30 am with a cup of tea in hand, looking forward to connecting with people who want and need the information I have to offer. Each day I make 40 calls – 10 to 15 to connect with my current clients and answer their questions,

and 25 to 30 calls to prospective investors. I feel relaxed and energized as I talk with people about creating a secure financial future.

Cory imagined feeling confident not just about his technical skill, but also about his ability to collaborate with people and deal with tricky customers. As part of this process, he had to ask himself some difficult questions. Did he prefer solitude during the workday, or did he secretly long to feel more comfortable in conversation? Did he want to eventually direct larger, more collaborative projects, or would he feel more comfortable reporting to someone else and working more or less solo? Should he stretch himself in his current position, or look for a new job that was a better match for his style of working?

Cory realized that his desire to feel comfortable and confident around people was more important than the details of his working environment. For that reason, he decided that, instead of pushing back against the new demands of his supervisors, he would embrace them. Here is some sample language that addressed Cory's *feeling* as much as his action:

I enjoy being around people. On the way to my office each morning, I comfortably greet people in the hallway. In meetings, I listen to other people's ideas and find something positive to say about their efforts. I speak up when I see a better way to approach a problem. At lunch, I join my colleagues for small talk. Whether I'm talking with just one person or in a group, it seems that I always have something to say. At night, I drift off to sleep easily, knowing that my job is secure.

Sandra imagined a relationship filled with the warmth and laughter she remembered from earlier times with Jay. Her vision included backpacking and beach trips, as well as parenting like a team. She wrote about couple time, family time, kid time, and personal time. Sandra wasn't sure how all that was going to fit together in real life, but there was easily room for it in her vision. She used this kind of language:

> *We finish work at 5:30 pm, and take 30 minutes to review our day, express our appreciation for each other's contribution, and plan the next day. Each weeknight, one family member cooks a delicious and healthful dinner. The rest of us organize the kitchen and set the table. We spend at least 30 minutes at the dinner table, with the conversation focused on each person's activities and plans. The conversation is fun and respectful. Before I speak, I take a moment to think about what I want to say, and make sure that I say it in a positive way. After dinner, we clean the kitchen together. Then Jay and I take a half-hour walk in the hills near our house.*

Exercise 5.4

Now go back to your own vision. Add enough detail to give it form, to personalize it, and make it more likely to come about. Use these questions to help add specifics.

+ ***Who*** *is part of your day? Who do you talk or work or spend evening time with? Do you have colleagues? Clients? Do you spend evenings with your friends, kids, or partner?*

+ ***What*** *do you do? Do you work at home, at an office, or on the road? What is your role? Do you own your own business or work for someone else? What kind of money do you make? If you're a full-time parent, then parenting is your work. If your goal is personal, what kinds of projects occupy your time?*

+ ***Where*** *is your home or your office? What does it look like? If you work from home, do you have a room, or at least a corner, to use for this purpose?*

+ ***When*** *do you start your day? When does it end? How many hours do you work? When do you take breaks? What does your daily routine look like?*

+ **Why** would you make these choices? How are they connected with your values, your skills, and your passions?

+ **How** do you feel about what you do in your vision?

· ·

Keeping It Positive

In general, it's easier to start something than to stop it. Consider these examples: Don't think of an elephant. Don't get mad. Don't space out. Don't take work home.

These intentions can be hard to live up to for a couple reasons. First, you have a vivid picture of what you don't want already distracting you. Second, a broad goal can be difficult to gauge. For instance, how do you know when you're not mad? Does irritated count? How about annoyed? It's much more helpful to look at positive, specific behavior. For example, you could change the anger-related goal to "speak in a calm voice," and it would be easier to tell when you're doing it.

When you imagine something, your mind paints an image of it. When you think about not eating ice cream, not waiting until the last minute, or not spending hours on the computer, what mental pictures do you notice? For most people, the images are of ice cream, procrastination, and spending too much time on the computer – the very things you want to stop doing. On the other hand, when you think about what you want to do – such as eating fruits and vegetables, starting on a task as soon as it's handed to you, or relaxing with your family – the goal is the image you're left with.

Here's a part of what Alexi, Cory, and Sandy started with:

Alexi: I don't procrastinate with the phone calls I need to make.

Cory: I don't avoid people at work.

Sandra: Jay and I never argue.

The "negatives" are a good starting point, but these statements are hardly inspiring. The revised versions looked like this:

Alexi: I start making calls at 8:30 am every morning.

Cory: I have at least five small, positive conversations with my colleagues every day.

Sandra: Jay and I speak calmly and respectfully.

The newer, positive language pointed these clients directly toward what they wanted. So imagine what you can do, instead of focusing on what you cannot. Look through the draft of your ideal day for words like "don't," "not," and "never." Change the wording to reflect what you want, so you're more likely to move toward it.

Exercise 5.5

· ·

Look through your vision for negative words and turn them to positive ones.

· ·

Imagining the Impossible

The best goals are just outside your comfort zone. They might even seem impossible – *at least at first*. With inspiration, resources, and commitment, though, people have found ways to overcome the most difficult of challenges. My clients have started businesses during difficult economic times, resolved challenging work situations, and negotiated tension-filled relationships. In fact, we are more likely to accomplish challenging goals than mundane ones. Challenging goals improve performance and help you learn. They stretch you as a person and help you accomplish things you never thought you could do. They build both confidence and skills.

Psychologists Edwin A. Locke and Gary P. Latham studied goal-setting as it affects motivation, performance, and work satisfaction. One of the things they found was that difficult goals are generally more motivating.

A challenging goal, they argue, helps you focus and inspires you to give it your best effort. And once you've made a commitment, you're more likely to persist if the goal in front of you is challenging.[4]

Sometimes the thrill is in the challenge itself. For example, "weekend warriors" are dedicated athletes with day jobs. They make up about 2% of the U.S. population,[5] and spend their "off time" working out. This group includes triathletes, marathon runners, and bicycle racers. Most of them would love to win, but few do. After all, training is not their full-time job. Over half a million people ran a marathon in 2011, yet there were less than a thousand official winners.[6]

When athletes are told something is impossible, the challenge makes them all the more dedicated. It was "impossible" for a woman to swim the 35-mile English Channel, until Gertrude Ederle swam it in 1926. In another arena, everyone "knew" that breaking the sound barrier was impossible, until pilot Chuck Yeager did it in 1947. Challenging goals are inspiring, and imagining them in vivid detail is a powerful first step toward them.

We need something to aspire to in life. People who set targets high feel more motivated and accomplish more. John F. Kennedy said in a speech at Rice University:

> We choose to go to the moon in this decade and do the other things, not because they are easy, but because they are hard, because that goal will serve to organize and measure the best of our energies and skills, because that challenge is one that we are willing to accept, one we are unwilling to postpone, and one which we intend to win, and the others, too.[7]

Kennedy emphasized setting our sights high, even if there is no guarantee that we'll get to our destination, because that's the kind of challenge that inspires us. Challenging goals encourage you to think creatively, find support, challenge your thinking, and expand your skills. The path to a challenging goal is rarely simple and obvious. To get there, you'll need to do things you've never done before, things you aren't aware of now.

A challenging goal is worthy of your time, focus, and energy. Your path to reach it probably won't be a straight one. But, as with the weekend warriors, the most challenging goals leave you feeling inspired.

Keeping Your Vision in Mind

The steps to change might be simple, but they're not always fast. You'll often encounter distractions, obstacles, and roadblocks. It helps if you can give your vision form, so that it can serve as a reminder of where you're headed.

Sandra, for example, used her old photos for inspiration. She and Jay met because they shared a love of the outdoors, and Sandra especially remembered a rare weekend backpacking trip in the Rocky Mountains. They wandered off the beaten path and ended up at a clear, sparkling, alpine lake. For hours, they enjoyed the wildflowers, the crystal waters, and the top-of-the-world view. Sandra remembered a tremendous sense of peace and spaciousness. The memory brought tears to her eyes. She wanted to recapture that feeling. Sandra framed that photo and put it up in a hallway where she would see it often.

When you find a symbol by writing, drawing, or choosing an object to represent your vision, you're creating a tangible reminder of your goal and your dreams. It helps you remember that out of all the possible paths you could travel, this one is the most inspiring, most compelling, and most meaningful to you at this time.

Exercise 5.6

Identify something tangible that represents the change you want to make to remind yourself of what you're working toward. You might decide to write your vision, then read it to yourself every day. You could find an object to represent your vision, like Sandra did, or you can create a collage, a sketch, or a recording to use as a reminder.

Imagination is a powerful beginning, but you'll need more. You'll need an effective, practical way to make your vision real. If imagining is your compass, then planning is the way to create a detailed map to your destination. In the next chapter, you'll learn how to take your vision and transform it into a concrete, do-able plan.

Key Points

+ Imagining can activate new pathways in your brain and help you accomplish new things.

+ In some circumstances, the brain doesn't distinguish between mental and physical practice.

+ Creating a vision of change – one that taps into your values and is compelling, vivid, positive, detailed, and challenging – creates inspiration for moving toward your goal.

Simple Actions to Develop Imagination

+ Read your vision every day, preferably aloud, to keep yourself inspired.

+ Keep a list of things you'd like to try someday.

+ Read to expand your thinking and challenge your point of view.

+ Change the script. When you think, *"That isn't possible,"* change that to *"What would it take to make that possible?"*

+ Try something new. Volunteer to give a presentation. Learn to cook pastries. Write a short story. Do anything that challenges your assumptions about what you can do.

+ Imagine anything that gives you joy.

Chapter 6

Plan

*"If you don't know where you're going,
you'll end up someplace else."*

– Yogi Berra

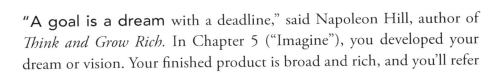

"A goal is a dream with a deadline," said Napoleon Hill, author of *Think and Grow Rich*. In Chapter 5 ("Imagine"), you developed your dream or vision. Your finished product is broad and rich, and you'll refer back to it often for inspiration.

When you move from the rich land of vision to the more mundane territory of deadlines and due dates, you begin to give your dream form. The bridge between a dream and a deadline is a specific plan with steps to point the way. The first step in doing this is to translate your vision back into specific, well-defined *goals*. Your plan is the path you'll travel to accomplish those goals.

From Vision to Goals

A goal is a clear statement of some *aspect* of your vision. It might resemble one of the goals you noted in Exercise 5.2, now backed by an inspiring vision. Or the process of writing your vision might have changed that goal. Either way, it needs to be *well-defined* so you can tell whether you're making progress, and when you've met it.

Let's look at the differences between vague and clear goals using one of Sandra's goals from Chapter 5: *Jay and I speak calmly and respectfully.*

Although she described her evenings in some detail, the specifics are still unclear. How will Sandra know when she's met that goal? What will she do along the way? Sandra decided to start with this:

> *Jay and I can talk about our finances for half an hour without raising our voices. When we talk about finances, no matter what Jay says I'm going to pause before I respond, and ask myself these questions: (1) What do I really want to say right now? and (2) How can I say this calmly and respectfully?*

This type of well-defined goal is a good starting point for making an effective plan. The next step is to add a *deadline*, to anchor the goal to the real world. Without a specific target date, it's easy to leave tasks for "someday" or "when I get to it." Sandra added this to her goal.

> *I'll feel successful when we can have calm, respectful conversations about money every week for three months.*

Deadlines should be *realistic*, of course. When they're not, they become a source of stress. In contrast, creating deadlines thoughtfully can help *reduce* stress. In fact, deadlines are essential for productivity. When the time frame is reasonable, deadlines consistently help people reach their goals.

Deadlines do this because they help you focus, create a challenge, and inspire action. Sometimes a task that seems boring or routine can come to life once there is a deadline attached to it. I saw this in a small way when my son was in first grade and learning to add and subtract. He resisted arithmetic homework until his teacher started Mad Math Minute competitions – a chance to see how many problems a student could do in one minute. After that, it was a game. I was no longer asking my son to do homework – he was asking *me* to time him.

Read the examples below, and notice how a goal changes when clarity and a time frame are added.

Laura

Original: I am writing a memoir.

New: I complete a memoir by June of next year.

Alexi

Original: My business is profitable by the end of the year.

New: By November, my revenue is $10,000 a month.

Cory

Original: I feel comfortable talking with people at work.

New: I start conversations with at least five people a day for two weeks.

Exercise 6.1

Look back over the vision you created of your ideal day. Out of all the possible goals that are part of your vision, choose one. Write that goal as a single, clear sentence.

Exercise 6.2

Describe how you'll know that you have reached your goal. How can you make it more specific and well-defined? Add an estimated date for completion.

It's hard to imagine a cause more compelling than saving lives. For the Chilean miner rescue in 2010, thoughtful planning helped all 33 men return to safety. The goal was clear: the miners were about 700 meters down under hard rock, and the only way to get to them was to drill. But the rest wasn't so obvious. The typical drilling routines were too harsh – the men wouldn't have survived the effects of the 600-pound percussion hammer needed for the largest drill. Also, a drill might have hit a fault zone, hampering the effort, or a newly drilled hole might have collapsed.

Since there was little margin for error, the rescuers started by drilling three separate holes at different angles and in separate locations. Each hole was a separate part of the rescue operation, designed to address different potential problems. The successful plan, for example, used five small hammers attached to the drill instead of one, so the overall stress on rock was reduced. To test the rock and help prevent collapses, the rescuers drilled a small hole first, only 5 inches in diameter. They later reamed it into a larger 12-inch hole, and only after that did they enlarge the hole to the final 26-inch size needed to carry the miners up.

Plans often need to be adjusted or changed. A drill broke. The small size of the space that the miners occupied created health and psychological problems. Because they planned carefully, however, the rescue teams were able to look ahead, pull in support (including NASA in this case), and map a path to the finish. Sixty-nine days later, the miners were out. Even though plans changed, they were the basis of the rescue.

Looking for Milestones

To plan a path to your clear and timely goal, you'll need milestones – events that will mark your progress. Milestones are useful because progress is often hard to see.

I first noticed this several decades ago, when I worked on setting up mental health programs in elementary schools. For our programs, teachers selected students who were having a hard time in school. Typically these students turned in incomplete classwork, got low test scores, and stood around by themselves at lunch and recess. Not surprisingly, they described themselves as being "not very good at spelling" or as "not having friends."

After a few months in our program, the teachers rated the students' behavior once again. In some classrooms, there can be so much problematic behavior that it's hard to see small changes. However, the teachers were able to use specific milestones to rate the students' behavior, and they found that these students were turning in classwork, working independently, and talking to other kids at recess and lunch. The teachers were excited.

Yet when we asked these same students how they were doing, they would say, "I'm not very good at spelling" or "I don't have any friends." After months of progress, the students' self-perception remained the same. We realized then that part of our job was to help the students notice their own changes, and that they needed milestones too. We pointed out how they were joining in lunchtime games and showed them their old, incomplete assignments alongside the newer, more complete ones. "Completes assignments: check. Plays with other kids at lunch: check." Milestones helped students to see their progress too.

For some goals, milestones are fairly easy to identify. Let's look at my client David, for example. He was in his twenties, but sedentary. He had tried a number of things – walking, hiking, yoga, weights. Each time he tried something new, weeks passed. However, he couldn't tell if his exercise was making any difference, so he gave up.

Were David's attempts to get in shape fruitless? Muscle-building and aerobic conditioning were slow. How could he tell how far he'd come?

First, David established a clear fitness goal: run a 10k in less than an hour by the end of April. He even had a particular 10k in mind, and he paid the entry fee to solidify his commitment. Since his starting time for a 10k was about 75 minutes, David set milestones for running a 10k in 70, 65, and 60 minutes. These milestones made David's progress visible, and they gave him the confidence to keep working out.

People who do strength training write down how much weight they can lift and how many repetitions they can do. For weight loss, people often track calories consumed, changes in weight, measurements, or percent body fat. Even flexibility and improved energy can be measured. For Laura, the writer, milestones could have been measured in completed chapters, or number of words, or specific events like "complete a first draft."

Milestones are essential when a goal is relational. Otherwise progress can be almost invisible, and it is easily missed. In over 25 years of working with couples, I've found that when change happens, it almost always gets pushed immediately to the background.

Sandra said at one point, for example, that she would feel more supported if Jay would regularly help with dinner. Jay took her request seriously, and most days he made a point of helping. A few weeks later, Sandra commented that she and Jay weren't making progress. When I pointed out the dinner help, she said, "Sure, he helps with dinner, but that's basic. I'd expect that from a roommate. How would that help us feel closer?"

Her response might seem unappreciative, but the truth was that for her the change was almost invisible. Jay, on the other hand, had made a significant effort to respond to Sandra and change that particular part of his routine. It's true that this one change wasn't enough to turn around their relationship, but it was a move in the right direction. Fortunately, we'd identified shared dinner preparation as one of their milestones, and with some reflection, Sandra could see that the two of them really were on track and moving forward.

Sandra's response is a pretty common one, and it seems to reflect how our brains work. Our brains are in part problem-seeking machines. Once a problem has been solved, it recedes to the background and becomes "normal," and we're on to solving the next problem. Part of my job as a counselor is to help people notice changes as they're happening.

Some of Sandra's other milestones were: (1) go through a single argument-free day and (2) spend 5 hours of relaxed time with Jay within a single week. Once she and Jay had made it past a dozen or so of these milestones, their relationship started to feel very different.

There are several strategies you can use to identify and organize milestones. Try one or more of these:

1. **Next step planning:** For most people, this strategy is the most straightforward. Think about your goal, and ask yourself, "What is the first and smallest thing I'd notice that would let me know I'm making progress?" Sandra's goals above are a good example of Next Step Planning.

2. **Planning backwards:** This is a great strategy for projects with deadlines. Miles, a college student, used this to finish term papers on time. The last step in the process, for him, was to turn in the completed paper. Before that, Miles needed to (in reverse order): (1) complete a final draft, (2) write a first draft, (3) finish his research, and (4) outline his approach. Looking over this list helped Miles recognize that writing a paper isn't just about the hours spent writing. It helped him plan for the other tasks as well, and start far enough in advance to finish the paper comfortably by the deadline.

3. **Mind mapping:** If the project is complex, it might be easiest to first write your goal in the center of a blank piece of paper, then draw spokes radiating out from that center. Next, write one of your milestones along each spoke. List the *timeline* for each milestone at the end of the spoke. This helps get your ideas down on paper. Later on, you can put them in order by when you want to get them done.

Milestones define the *structure* of your plan. They keep you moving toward your goal, because they show you how today's effort will pay off. They add predictability, a sense of continuous movement, and the knowledge that you're on the right path. Each time you complete one, you get a sense of satisfaction and an expectation of further progress (for more on gaining a sense of satisfaction, see Chapter 9, "Celebrate").

When you look back, milestones remind you of where you've been. With that perspective, you have a better view of the changes you've made. By using milestones to make the invisible visible, you'll be on your way to shifting your self-perception and, because of that, your confidence.

Exercise 6.3
. . . .

Look over the goal you worked with in Exercise 6.1 and 6.2. Identify between two and eight identifiable events that could serve as milestones to mark your progress.

. . . .

Exercise 6.4
. . . .

Add target dates to your milestones.

. . . .

Getting Started with *Tasks*

Once you've identified the milestones, you're ready to start on the first leg of your journey. Take a look at your first milestone, and identify the particular *tasks* you need to get done. Tasks are the simple, easy-to-identify *actions* that you can complete in a few minutes or a few hours. These are the things that end up on your "to do" list. If you're going on a vacation, the tasks might include: (1) buying the ticket, (2) reserving a hotel, (3) renting a car, (4) planning the itinerary, and (5) making a packing list.

Tasks are the things that fill your day. Most people are juggling dozens or even hundreds of tasks, and new ones come up all the time. Your boss tells you that a funding proposal just came in and needs to be completed by tomorrow at noon. Your cat's sick and has to go the vet. Your son's school wants someone to bake brownies.

Because of this, it's essential to choose carefully when deciding which tasks to add to your calendar. Out of all the things that demand your attention, choose at least one that moves you a step closer to your goal. Choose a task that:

✦ Is the most important or will give the biggest result

✦ Will be the most fun or interesting

✦ Will fit into the amount of time you have

Exercise 6.5

Identify two to ten tasks – first steps that you could take in moving toward your goal.

Exercise 6.6

Choose one of these tasks and add it to tomorrow's calendar. How does it feel to have a clear path of action that leads you toward your goal and your vision?

Understanding Time

If you haven't been able to "manage" your time, you're not alone.

The truth is that time *can't* be managed – nor can it be created, squeezed, or stretched. Time is the background against which we work. It's the metaphorical suitcase for the stuff of our life. When you try to pack a suitcase too full, the contents eventually spill out and spread over the floor. There's only so much that will fit.

Since time doesn't flex, you need to be thoughtful about how you use it, by reserving space in your day, your week, and your life for the activities that really matter to you. Each week, you'll need to decide how much time to spend on your goal, which *tasks* will help you move toward it, and then schedule these on your *calendar.*

When I mention calendars, which I do often, people start to tune out. "I don't need a calendar," my clients assure me. "I have a good memory."

I'm sure there are some people, somewhere, who really don't need them. In reality, though, if you're too busy, too stressed, or aren't getting important things done, a calendar is essential. Calendars are tools that map the tasks you select onto the time that's available to you in a given day or week.

Here's how it works:

+ Each week, spend 15 minutes deciding how much time you'll spend on your most important projects.

+ Each morning, spend 5 minutes writing in the tasks you plan to do that day.

Make sure that the projects and tasks you choose are *easily* doable in the amount of time you have. Overestimate the time you think you'll need when you're starting something new, because it takes extra energy (and therefore extra time) if you're doing something that's not part of your usual routine. Whether you want to rethink your workday like Alexi, track your interactions like Cory, or respond differently to your spouse like Sandra, something will likely come up to take up some of the time you thought was "free."

Exercise 6.7

1. *Take 15 minutes at the start of your week to decide how many hours you'll spend this week working toward your goal. Write your answer, and come back to this question each week.*

2. *Take 5 minutes to decide when, tomorrow, you can schedule time for the tasks you identified in Exercise 6.5. Write your answer, and come back to this question every day.*

Doing More by Doing Less

Downtime is an essential part of any plan. Whether you're keeping track of energetic children or managing a high-pressure job, you need periods of rest throughout the day. When people say things like "I don't stop for a minute all day," "I always work through lunch," or "I don't have time to take a vacation," I know that they're likely to have trouble with productivity, stress, or both. On the other hand, *doing less* can make it more likely that you'll accomplish your goal.

Working for long periods without a break is inefficient. The longer you work, the more energy you expend, and as you continue to spend energy, your ability to focus decreases. You need a way to *replenish*.

Just as elite athletes schedule recovery periods and days off, you need to schedule downtime in order to stay at your peak. Overdoing training leads to sports injuries, and in a similar way, non-stop working results in mental "wheel-spinning" and can lead to illness.

First a word about *what downtime isn't*: it's not emailing, texting, making phone calls, writing down your grocery list, or addressing your wedding invitations. It isn't filing, clearing your desk, or "catching up." Downtime is simply a period of *no task-oriented activity.*

Downtime *can* include talking with a friend, spending time with your family, or spending relaxed time by yourself. It includes not just time in the evening and on weekends, but also space between tasks at work. Research shows that people who take breaks do better. Studies found that short breaks improve job performance for nurses[1] and airline pilots,[2] for example.

Research by the Boston Consulting Group (BCG), summarized in the *Harvard Business Review,* found that "predictable time off" led to better work, more collaboration, and more efficiency.[3] In particular, downtime helps you solve problems by allowing connections to develop between seemingly unrelated parts of your life. Those connections often spur new thoughts about how to approach the things you're working on.

If downtime is so helpful, why don't people create more of it? One reason is the general belief, especially in the U.S., that *more is better.* New research, such as the BCG findings above, is just beginning to challenge that belief. Another reason downtime is underused is that it can leave us vulnerable to worries and fears that we're not sure how to handle. "I stay busy so I'm not lonely," one of my clients said to me. Another client shared: "When I start to dwell on the past, I jump into my work." If you're a person who has a hard time feeling comfortable with downtime, some of the strategies in Chapter 4 ("Pause") can help.

Time is a resource. We have only so much of it, and how and when we choose to spend it greatly impacts our lives. Time doesn't stretch or shrink. It's not something that you need to "race against," but rather something that, if used wisely, can help you get things done faster and with less distraction.

If you get good at scheduling downtime, you're likely to excel. Like an athlete, the periods of rest will help you perform at your peak more often.

Exercise 6.8

. . . .

1. *Schedule downtime in your week. Include it on your calendar, where you will see it: blocks of time for relaxation, play, yoga, or just staring out the window. Even if this downtime isn't directly related to your plan, it will help you accomplish it.*

2. *Schedule extra time. Make sure there is enough unscheduled time in your schedule for you to handle unexpected difficulties, low energy days, and other interruptions that will inevitably come up.*

. . . .

Resisting Randomness

Without a detailed plan, *randomness* will nudge most people back into their old ways. For a plan to be effective, you'll need to understand how randomness in your day affects your ability to get things done.

You might think you've been working on a report "all day." However, if you're like most people, the reality is different. There were 37 emails, five phone calls, three quick questions from colleagues, four texts about tomorrow afternoon's meeting, a phone call about the barbecue next weekend, and the web surfing you did to give yourself "a break." Those interruptions are examples of the random forces in your day, which can contribute to feelings of burnout.

For Alexi, this was the single biggest obstacle to reorganizing her day. She was interrupted constantly – by clients of course, but also by colleagues, staff, and the few dozen tasks that came her way every day. She was choosing to allow those interruptions, without any organized approach for managing them. This "putting out fires" approach was adding tension and slowing her down.

Setting-goals and holding firm with priorities in the midst of a busy life can be a challenge for anyone. For someone who already has trouble with focus and attention, it can feel almost impossible. A clear, well-thought-out, detailed plan is what makes it possible.

Over the next few weeks, Alexi and I looked at her days – not at first with the idea of getting more things done or being more efficient. Instead, we looked at her process for making choices, and how those choices impacted her schedule, success, and sense of well-being.

Here's one example of the planning that Alexi and I did together: *scheduling her email.*

Email is probably the biggest creator of inefficiency in a workday. One study suggested that email costs businesses something like $8,000 per employee per year, for a company with 3,000 employees.[4] The inefficiency comes from time going back and forth between email and other tasks, reading messages that should have been sent to someone else, re-reading messages that you didn't have time to respond to the first time, and so forth.

The biggest energy drain comes from stopping the task that you're already doing to check your email. One study followed workers for three and half days, and it found that when people responded to email and other interruptions, they switched tasks about every 3 minutes. After the switch, they tended to move on to new tasks and only return to their original task after an average of 23 minutes.[5] These data suggest that people spend enormous amounts of valuable time and energy just switching between tasks caused by interruptions.

Alexi's solution was to *plan.* She set specific hours to check her email and clear her in-box. *Outside of* those hours, she closed her email program. *During* those hours, she stopped her practice of handling the easy messages and leaving the difficult ones to pile up. Instead, she reserved enough time to go through each item and (1) take care of it, (2) delegate it, (3) delete it, or (4) schedule it for another time.

This system cut her email time from almost 3 hours a day to about 90 minutes, including the time needed to handle the prior day's email requests. That means she gained an extra 90 minutes a day of unscheduled time, or about an extra 360 hours a year – just from a planned approach to the randomness of email!

One by one, Alexi and I peeled back the layers of randomness, and we helped her develop new habits in a way that would stick. As she started to make more conscious choices, her workday started to reflect the life Alexi wanted for herself.

Exercise 6.9

. . . .

Although scheduling email might not be directly related to your plan, it will help you stick to your plan. Schedule a regular time each day to empty your e-mail in-box and schedule the actionable tasks.

. . . .

The Power of Writing

German philosopher Friedrich Nietzsche said that "the most basic form of human stupidity is forgetting what we are trying to accomplish." Putting your plans in writing helps you *remember*. Without a written plan, your immediate goal can get lost in the dozens of things you typically juggle.

Milestones, too, help you notice progress when they are *written down* and *tracked*. In general, writing has a track record when it comes to helping people accomplish goals, as evidenced by a study by Gail Matthews at Dominican University.[6] She recruited 267 subjects from business groups in the U.S. and asked them to set goals. The goals focused on a variety of work-related issues, such as income, productivity, stress, and work/life balance. The group that just set goals accomplished 43% of them. As the level of commitment and accountability increased, so did the success rate. The group that wrote their goals down and shared their progress met 67% of their goals.

On a related note, statistics on New Year's resolutions suggest that people who make their resolutions explicit (and what better way to make them explicit than by putting them on paper) are 10 times more likely to attain them.[7]

It's one thing to daydream about writing a book or making more money. It's another to create a written action plan for exactly how you're going to get your first draft of a novel written in 30 days or the specific activities you'll need to raise your salary by $30,000 in the next 6 months.

The time it takes to put words that make sense on paper will save you hundreds of hours later on. You'll be more inspired and more likely to stay on track. You'll also be clearer about your target and less likely to be diverted by other enticing opportunities.

A large 2012 survey by ComPsych Corp found that 63% of employees report high levels of work stress. They feel tired and out of control. In some cases, other employees, job structure, and personal difficulties beyond their control are the culprits.[8] For many, interestingly, a large contributing factor is a difficulty in seeing *the results* of their efforts. Writing down your goals and your plan to achieve them helps make those results clear.

Activity in itself isn't achievement. It's not how much you do during the day that matters; it's whether you're moving toward your goals. If your plan isn't written and you don't have a deadline, then your goal is still just a dream.

Exercise 6.10

· ·

If you've been doing the exercises, you've been putting your plan in writing as you've read this chapter. If you haven't, then go through the chapter exercises now. Then print your plan, and place it where you can refer to it easily and often.

· ·

Once you have a plan, you have a path. You're well on your way toward turning your vision into reality. Plans change and grow with you, of course. People will help you move forward more quickly, or they'll hold you back. Events will transpire to get in your way or clear your path. Making adjustments is a constant, expectable part of the process of moving toward your dreams. The bottom line is this: Plans help you take the necessary action, make changes, gather support, and move forward.

In Chapter 7 ("Shrink"), you'll learn what to do when you don't feel motivated, and how to fine-tune your plan by making your next steps smaller, simpler, and easier.

Key Points

+ Effective planning starts with a clear goal and a deadline.

+ Creating milestones makes your progress visible and therefore faster.

+ Scheduling your tasks is key to moving forward.

+ Downtime increases productivity and efficiency.

+ Writing a plan maximizes your chance of success.

Simple Actions to Help with Planning

+ **Prioritize.** *Spend 15 minutes a week planning your week's activities, so the important things get done first.*

+ **Save time.** *Spend 5 minutes each morning working out your schedule for the day. This simple habit has saved many of my clients over an hour a day. It's an invaluable habit for everyone and essential for people who have difficulties with focus and attention.*

+ **Create milestones.** Each time you plan a path to a new goal, identify between two and eight milestones to mark your progress along the way.

+ **Reflect.** As you add each task to your daily plan ask yourself, "Do I have time to finish this today given all the other things I've agreed to do?"

Include in your plan simple actions that provide the energy and perspective you need to follow through.

+ Schedule at least two breaks during your workday.

+ Schedule at least an hour twice a week for yourself to play, relax, or have fun.

+ Schedule regular time in your week to connect with at least one person who is important to you – your partner, child, parent, neighbor, or friend.

Chapter 7

Shrink

"It is better to take many small steps in the right direction than to make a great leap forward only to stumble backward."

– Proverb

It's energizing to think big: Change jobs. Find a new partner. Take a month off. Create a new strategy. Move to a new city.

Yet big changes have small origins. Small changes in how you say something can affect the outcome of an important conversation. Small changes in organization can free hours of time at work. When you learn to swim, you don't just dive into the deep end. You start by blowing bubbles. Almost everything big starts small.

There are a few compelling reasons why moving ahead in small steps is wise:

1. **Your life is already full.** You have work to do, relationships to nurture, chores to take care of. Let's say that your goal is to get more exercise. It's not like you're pacing the floor for an hour every evening, wondering what to do with that extra time, waiting for this moment of inspiration: "Yes! *This* is the hour I'll use for exercise!" Instead, you have plans, commitments, and obligations. This means that new plans and projects can easily fall by the wayside.

2. **Change will be harder than you think.** Simple doesn't necessarily mean easy. It's impossible to see perfectly into the future. Things won't go the way you expect, and you'll need more time and more energy than you think to make a change. You'll need some extra time to deal with internal resistance, changing circumstances, and unforeseen obstacles.

It might seem obvious that you're more likely to carry out small changes than big ones. Even so, most people find it hard to think small. There are several reasons for this. First, when you're excited or under pressure, small actions might not seem big *enough*. Filing one paper makes only the tiniest dent in the stacks covering your desk. However, if your filing is part of a new *system*, and you file another paper *each time* you sit down at your desk, you're well on your way to desk organization.

Second, doing something small can feel like you're settling. Sandra, for example, started by inviting her husband Jay on a 10-minute walk. What she really wanted was *hours* of conversation, affection, and fun. At first, it was hard for her to notice the positive effect of those few minutes, because she kept thinking about how much more she wanted. It took months before she realized that this small action was key in shifting the *tone* of their relationship. *That* eventually led to more time.

Third, it's hard to see small progress. When change is small, visible results can take weeks or months to appear. For example, it takes more than a few minutes of mindfulness (see Chapter 4, "Pause") to reduce your stress or improve your focus. Yet research shows that practicing mindfulness for a few minutes a day, over time, brings lasting improvement. While you're waiting to see results, knowing that there's plenty of research showing the benefits of mindfulness can give you the confidence to continue.

Despite these issues, small change is the most likely way – and sometimes the only way – to make big changes. Let's look at why this is true.

Why Small Is Powerful

Greek mathematician Archimedes once said, "Give me a lever long enough and a place to stand, and I can move the Earth." The function of a lever is to reduce the force needed to move something large or heavy. In that sense, small actions play the role of levers that nudge you slowly but consistently toward your goals.

Small actions help get you started, and *getting started* is the key to getting things done. From there, *any* small step that moves you forward is progress. If the big report due in a week feels daunting, make your goal to write one paragraph... or just the first sentence. If you're working on a big presentation, write down one point you'd like to make.

Small actions also build *momentum*. Once you've started a task, you'll feel an urge to finish it. This difficulty in letting go of an unfinished task is called the *Zeigarnik effect*,[1] named after Bluma Zeigarnik – the Russian psychologist who first suggested the phenomenon. She observed that people remember the details of incomplete tasks better than those of completed tasks, and that this creates an impulse to get back to the incomplete task. This is great news. Once you start something new, you'll feel an urge to finish it – *if* it's small enough to feel manageable in the time you have.

Starting small also makes complex change manageable. It's easier to improve your productivity, health, or relationship when you focus on small actions or small amounts of time. When you can't find extra time, do something that takes *less* time. When you find yourself postponing things "until tomorrow," it's a clue that the project is too large. Instead of going to the gym in the morning for a long workout, walk for 20 minutes during your lunch break. If you have even less time, start with a 5 minute walk, or just step outside for a breath of fresh air. Small actions aren't "settling." Rather, they are ways to create a big "later" from a smaller "now."

It's better to accomplish something small than to leave a bigger task undone. B.J. Fogg, Ph.D., Director of Stanford University's Persuasive Technology Lab, suggests making small, specific changes that take *30 seconds or less*... and repeating them every day. Small can mean memorizing three words of a new language, or writing one sentence of a story, or giving your partner a hug. If you find yourself resisting the action you've planned, he says, don't push through. Instead, make the change *even smaller.*

Make your actions so small, in fact, that the change feels almost effortless. Instead of avoiding a half-hour of guitar practice (you're doing this because you enjoy it, presumably), play three cords and then pat yourself on the back for a job well done. Instead of avoiding a networking event, have a one-minute conversation with just one person. Enter one number into your spreadsheet, or do one push-up. Practice one musical scale. Run around one block.

Let's consider how to shrink the goals listed in Chapter 2 ("Why Most Resolutions Fail") under Reason 4 ("You Rely Too Much on Willpower").

+ **Before:** I'm going to spend every Friday night with my family.

+ **After:** Right after dinner tonight, I'm going to set up *Bannanagrams* and invite everyone to play.

+ **Before:** I'm going to lose 20 pounds by the end of June.

+ **After:** I'm going to start lunch tomorrow by eating a piece of fruit.

+ **Before:** I'm going to run three times a week starting Tuesday morning.

+ **After:** I'm going to change from my work clothes into my running clothes as soon as I get home tonight.

The "after" actions each take very little time – less than 5 minutes. They don't solve the problem entirely, but they do get you started. Now you're on a path toward change.

Exercise 7.1

Consider the change you most want to make. Choose from the milestones and tasks you listed in Chapter 6. What action could you take to move toward that change in:

- ✦ *20 minutes*
- ✦ *5 minutes*
- ✦ *30 seconds*

Don't Stop – Replace!

It's hard to stop doing something. Try this, for example: *Don't think of a giraffe. Don't look up. Don't argue.* What does a non-giraffe look like? What do you do when you're not arguing? When you think about something, your mind starts planning how to do it, which makes thinking of alternatives more difficult. Stopping a behavior requires willpower – and as we've discussed, willpower is unreliable.

Instead of stopping, think about *replacing* a behavior that you don't like. Let's say you want to stop snacking on chips in the afternoons. That takes willpower, and you're trying to use it late in the day when you have little willpower left. This will make your chip-eating behavior hard to stop. Instead, you might *replace* it with a healthier behavior, like eating a piece of fruit or sipping a cup of tea.

Most people have to experiment with simple actions to see which ones are most effective in replacing an old behavior. To stop working through lunch, you might make a small change to interrupt your flow of work – such as standing up and stretching when the clock says noon. To change the "chips" habit, you could leave the chips at the store, or buy a smaller single-serving sized package. The need to get to the store for each pack of chips replaces the old pattern of simply reaching for them.

When you want to replace an action, it's easiest if you can find a new action that accomplishes the *same immediate goal*. For example, when you snack, your immediate goal might be to relieve stress. If eating gives comfort, then replacing chips with a healthy snack might serve the same purpose with the added benefit of being more nutritious.

Exercise 7.2

. . . .

a. Is there a habit or a routine you would like to stop? If so, write it down.

b. What might be the positive purpose of that habit? From what perspective would this habit make perfect sense – if it only worked? Some possibilities are: to relieve stress, provide comfort, to feel closer to someone, to create a sense of safety, to release energy.

c. What small action could serve that purpose instead?

. . . .

Focus on Action

Small change is *specific*. We've already looked at how a plan can turn a powerful vision into a series of actions. *Shrinking* the actions continues this process. For example, a plan might be to make 40 client calls every weekday, starting today. If you can do it, great. If it feels overwhelming, though, you'll accomplish more in the long run if you shrink it. The smaller version might look like this: "I'm going to call Doug Smith tomorrow morning at 8:45." The end result is an action – something you can do right away.

Let's look at how to transform some other goals into specific small actions:

+ **Before:** Spend an hour a week with a friend.

+ **After:** Have lunch with Janine on Tuesday.

- **Before:** Organize the kitchen.
- **After:** Put all the pots in the lower right-hand cupboard.

- **Before:** Be more affectionate.
- **After:** Give my son a hug.

- **Before:** Save more money.
- **After:** Transfer $100 this Friday from my checking to my savings account.

- **Before:** Build confidence.
- **After:** Introduce myself to one new person this afternoon.

You can turn any goal into a small action or a series of small actions. Thinking small encourages a lot of *practice*, and the more you practice the better you'll get. This is not only true for skills, like playing the piano or learning a language. It's also true for any type of change, from building confidence to rejuvenating a relationship.

Cory, for example, used small actions to build his comfort in talking with people. He decided to talk with three people a day. This could take the form of a greeting, a comment in a meeting, or a question about someone's project. His small actions, over time, gave Cory the skills to start facilitating meetings with clients. His gains were not from Cory trying harder or "pushing through," but rather from making each new action small enough to feel easy.

Make Small Actions More Powerful

You can increase the effectiveness of small action in two ways: (1) write them down and (2) share them with someone.

As discussed in Chapter 6 ("Plan"), people with written goals are more likely to achieve them. Putting your small actions in writing helps you focus on them, clarifies what exactly you plan to do, and motivates you to take action.

It also helps to have a partner with whom you can share your progress. As Cory practiced starting conversations with people, it helped that there were *two* of us tracking his experience. In his case, it was easier for me to notice his developing skill and confidence than it was for him to observe his own changes. When you're trying to meet a new goal, it can help to recruit a partner with whom you can share your small actions. Not only will they hold you accountable and cheer you on, but they'll also help you notice your progress.

Examples of Small Change

Among the most common goals in the U.S. are promises to save more money, improve relationships, and overcome fears. Below are examples of how some of my clients tackled these particular problems with small actions. More simple actions are suggested at the end of the chapter.

Saving Money

Marie, a recently divorced mother of three, was struggling with her new life as a single mom. A divorce is difficult both emotionally and practically, but it's also hard on another level. There's the loss of a dream, of the vision of what you hoped for and what might have been.

As we talked, Marie told me about one of her regrets. "I know this is going to sound crazy," she said. "I mean, there are so many problems I still have to solve and things I have to do that it seems almost trivial. But there is something we planned that will never happen now."

As Marie talked, I thought about how wishes for the future are often important symbolically. They carry hope and energy, and these wishes can help people get through hard times. I encouraged her to keep talking.

"It's that I've always wanted to take my kids to New York," she said. "I know what's really important for my kids is our family and their friends and their school. Still, New York is one of the most exciting places I've ever been, and I promised myself that someday I'd take them there. Now there's no way I can afford it." She sighed.

We sat for a while with her disappointment. Then I suggested, "What if you put your spare change in a 'New York jar,' and see how much you have after a year or two." Four years later, Marie spent two weeks in New York with her three kids. The trip was funded by her spare change.

Improving Relationships

Simple actions can improve relationships with colleagues, employers, family members, friends, or a marriage partner. In turn, the quality of your relationships affects your physical and mental health, as well as how long you live. This happens because simple actions can reduce stress, provide support, and help develop a sense of meaning and purpose.[2]

Relationships are powerful, but the actions that build them are small. Positive, relationship-building moments don't have to be huge or long-lasting, but they do need to be frequent. For greater well-being, what matters is how often people experience positive feelings, rather than how intense those feelings are.[3] Barbara Fredrickson persuasively argues this point in her book, *Love 2.0*. Love, she says, isn't about big life events – a fabulous honeymoon, an over-the-top date, a spectacular gift. Love is about the tiny *moment-to-moment interactions* you have with your partner, the simple things you say and do all day long.[4] There are possibilities for change hidden in every moment.

Sandra wanted to stop the arguing in the relationship with her husband. To do this, she made the simple (but difficult!) commitment to stay quiet and listen to Jay's argument before putting forth her own views. She created a series of small actions to help her do this: (1) take a deeps breaths, (2) repeat back his point of view, (3) check to see if she understood what he was trying to say, and (4) give her point of view if she could say it calmly.

She resolved to try this for one week. The breath would give her a few moments to think about how... and *if...* she wanted to respond. That extra 5 seconds helped Sandra stay present. It helped her decide whether to respond right away, or take some time to think. It helped her choose words that might make a real difference in how she and Jay talked with each other. This simple action gave Sandra choices about her own biochemistry and about her relationship. Here's what the change in conversation looked like:

Old Conversation

Jay: "You make me feel like a kid when you tell me how to clean up the kitchen."

Sandra: "I don't make you feel anything, and if you're going to put things in random places so it's impossible to cook, then I'm going to say something about it."

Jay: "There you go with that tone again."

Sandra: "What tone? I'm trying to make a simple point!"

Jay: "I'm not going to talk about this anymore." (He leaves the room.)

New Conversation

Jay: "You make me feel like a kid when you tell me how to clean up the kitchen."

Sandra: (breath) "I didn't realize – I'll pay attention to how I word things."

Jay: "Good."

This simple change wasn't easy, and of course it wasn't a solution. Sandra had to manage her feelings, and she had to resist the urge to explain, defend, or fight back. With coaching and determination, it took her a few weeks to get good at it. However, it was a start, and the benefits were huge. First, their arguments stopped. It's impossible to have an argument when only one person is participating. Second, Jay's behavior started to change. His tone went from angry, to grumpy, then finally to calm.

Does every relationship change when one person responds differently? Unfortunately, no. But it happens surprisingly often, and it did for this couple. For Sandra and Jay, letting go of arguments was part of the beginning of major relationship change.

Overcoming a Fear of Heights

Joe was afraid of heights. "It's scary to be on the edge of stuff," he told me 5 years ago. "Even a hill or a road with a steep drop-off is a problem."

Fear of heights, or acrophobia, is an irrational fear of high or exposed places. For some people, a cliff is a high place. For others, a high place means standing on a chair or even a single step of a staircase.

The word irrational is important, because it *does* make sense to notice how far you are from the ground. Falls can be dangerous, even deadly, and it's prudent to be cautious. However, we're not born with a fear of heights. In fact, infants appear to be curious, rather than afraid, when presented with a drop-off. Basically, the fear of heights is a rational fear taken to an irrational level.

Joe could have simply avoided high, exposed places, as many people do. But some friends dragged Joe to a gym with a good rock climbing wall, and right away he loved the climbing. Joe wanted to learn more, and he was determined not to let his fear get in the way.

It was hard at first. He said, "I would get most of the way up a pitch, and I would be stuck there because I got scared. Even if it was a competition, I would freeze."

Many climbers, it turns out, are afraid of heights. In that sense, Joe was in good company when he decided to continue climbing anyway. His strategy was to go as far as he could up each pitch. When Joe reached his height limit, he stayed on the wall for a while, then came down and repeated the process. He wasn't concerned with how high he went – only that the height was a challenge for him. Joe kept climbing the same pitches over and over until he felt more comfortable.

"I had to push myself," he said. "It took a while, but eventually heights started to feel normal."

The method Joe discovered is at the heart of *exposure therapy*. When we're anxious, our natural tendency is to *avoid* whatever is causing the anxiety. Exposure therapy, on the other hand, allows you to *approach* what you fear little by little, each time challenging yourself a tiny bit more. This technique helps people with social anxiety, fear of public speaking, fear of flying, and a variety of other fears. This type of treatment is very successful in situations where medication typically isn't all that effective.

Joe's strategy enabled him to stretch himself, but in ways that were small and manageable. This strategy helped Joe do more than climb rock walls, because he was operating from a fundamental principle. How we do a small thing is how we do everything.

"Climbing a wall might not seem like much to other people," he said, "but to me what mattered is that I kept pushing myself. I realized then that I could use the same strategy to get over other fears, like being in crowds and talking in front of groups of people. You have to keep trying, and little by little you'll get there. You can use that strategy for anything."

Overcoming a Fear of Public Speaking

Certainly the vast majority of people rank stage fright as number one – 75% according to the National Institutes of Mental Health. For some people, this means a fear of speaking to large groups. For others, it means speaking to even a single person if that person has the power to evaluate you, as in a supervisor, interviewer, or professor giving an oral exam.

My client Robert had a new job that required him to give presentations. He had avoided public speaking for years, but the new job was his incentive to finally address the fear. Fortunately, he had about 6 months to get started. He got over his fear by building his audience one person at a time.

Robert started by giving "presentations" that lasted only a few minutes to a trusted colleague, and later to his supervisor. He then made his "presentation" longer and started to facilitate staff meetings. Six months later, with some coaching, he was speaking with confidence to groups of 50 people.

Big goals can be inspiring, and they give you something to aim for. However, if you're not making progress toward your goal, don't try harder. Instead, think smaller. Shrink your next step into a doable size. In the long run, it's the small changes that shape your life.

Now that you know how to shrink your actions, you'll want to know how to set them in motion. In Chapter 8 ("Act"), we'll look at how to turn small actions into habits so that they become part of what you do automatically.

Key Points

+ Big changes have small origins.
+ Small changes build momentum.
+ "Thinking small" makes it easy to practice, and the more you practice the better you'll get.
+ Positive relationships are built on the tiny moment-to-moment interactions you have with people.

Simple Actions that Improve Productivity

+ **Get organized.** To clear off your desk, file three papers a day. To finish a difficult report, write a paragraph a day. To reorganize your house, put away, give away, or throw away one thing each day. Joe and Marion used this strategy to cut in half the amount of "stuff" they owned. After two years, they had a clutter-free house and a much simpler lifestyle.

✦ **Simplify.** Unsubscribe from an email list you never read. Group all your phone calls and emails together to reduce distractions.

Simple Actions that Improve Relationships

✦ **Practice gratitude.** In one study, people wrote a few sentences each week about what they were grateful for. Ten weeks later, those people felt significantly more optimistic, had fewer medical problems, and exercised more.[5] Write one sentence a day about what you're grateful for.

✦ **Reach out.** Appreciate something. Give a hug. Give a kiss. Share a joke. Ask a question. Give a compliment. Ask about someone's day. Say "thank you."

Chapter 8

Act

*"I dream of men who take the next step
instead of worrying about the next thousand steps."*

– Theodore Roosevelt

You've learned to create small, do-able actions. The key to lasting change is to turn those actions into habits.

Habits help avoid the willpower problem, and as a result, they help you conserve mental and physical energy. You don't have to think through every one of your small actions every day. Instead, those actions become a part of your routine. We are all creatures of habit. An estimated 40% of the actions we take each day are automatic and outside of our awareness, which means that we live most of life by relying on habit.[1]

Beyond Willpower

When habits are positive, they help build excellence. The difference between a professional and an amateur in any field, argues *Turning Pro* author Steven Pressfield, is developing the right habits.[2] If you'd like to be more productive, for example, it's more important to make one phone call every day than it is to plan for 20, feel overwhelmed, and avoid them.

Here's why this is so important. When people make promises to themselves, they often rely on determination and self-control to bring about change. But self-control (another name for willpower) is unreliable. In fact, research shows that believing you have a lot of self-control makes habits harder to change. According to Northwestern University professor Loran Nordgren, most people overestimate their ability to resist problem behavior. In fact, often the "people who are the most confident about their self-control are the most likely to give into temptation."[3]

Habits also make your small actions easier to *remember*. Instead of needing to refer to a written list, you'll learn to link them to things you already do so they become automatic. This is important, because with any new behavior it's easy to get caught up in your usual routine and forget. Something unexpected will come up just as you were meaning to sit down and catch up on correspondence or leave for the gym. Then your *old habits* take over, and you end up doing whatever it is you usually do.

There are two parts to creating habits. They are:

1. Consistent action

2. A supportive environment

While it's not always possible to feel motivated, it *is* possible to develop consistent action and create a supportive environment. Tiny changes in your routines and environment can increase motivation to the point where taking action happens *simply and naturally*. Now motivation is something you can *create*.

We'll look at each of these components in turn.

Consistent Action

As noted, you can make your new actions consistent by *linking* them to something you already do. B.J. Fogg, head of Stanford's Persuasive Technology Lab, refers to this as a "trigger." Charles Duhig, author of *The Power of Habit*, calls it a "cue." Other habit experts agree that the secret to establishing habits is to integrate them into your existing routine. There are a number of ways you can do this. You can choose a particular time or place for your new small action, or you can link it to a regular event, a feeling, or even another simple action. Let's look at each of these.

Linking to a Time or a Place

For athletes and performers, consistent action means *practice.* Practice is the foundation of their ability to feel confident and accomplish their goals. One of the keys to successful practice is connecting it to *a particular time and place.* When I was in high school gymnastics, the coach never said, "This week you're all going to learn to do a backbend. Start practicing!" Instead, she was very specific. She said something like "Practice is at the gym Monday through Friday from 4:00 to 6:00 pm. Be there!"

Consistent action happens at a very *specific time.* If you use an actual time, like 6:00 am every weekday, you can set an alarm clock to remind you. If you're at your desk, you can schedule an electronic reminder via your computer or cell phone.

You don't have to be an athlete or performer to benefit from this kind of consistency. "Practice" time can be used to work on budgets, to write in a journal, or to change the way you're talking with your partner. The concept of practice can be applied to anything that helps to move you toward your goal. This means taking the simple actions you identified in Chapter 7 ("Shrink") and giving them a specific place in your routine. Linking it to a particular time and place helps link the new simple action to something you already do.

For example, Tonya decided to work on her resume and plan her networking every weekday, at her desk, from 10:00 am to noon. Over time Tonya got used to this routine, and she started to "feel like" working at those times.

This works because tasks that aren't part of your daily routine take mental energy and willpower, and as we have seen, these are exhaustible. When something becomes part of your routine – and therefore automatic, you no longer need to use valuable energy on remembering and deciding. Instead, the new action happens almost automatically. This is the way new habits are built.

Linking to Regular Events

Regular events are *specific actions* that happen every day or many times a day. These too can be links for building new habits. Some examples are:

+ Waking up
+ Getting out of bed
+ Getting in the car
+ Opening the front door
+ Opening your email program
+ Putting your toothbrush away

For example, remember Laura – the writer from Chapter 2 ("Why Most Resolutions Fail?") who said she wasn't motivated? Her task was simple enough: to write a paragraph each morning. However, it wasn't happening. "I can go through an entire morning and not get to it," she told me. "There are so many other things happening that I just forget."

This wasn't a memory problem per se. It was a problem of connecting the new routine to things she was already doing. Laura's solution was this: "As soon as I walk in the door after taking my kids to school, I'll sit down at my computer and write one sentence." For her, this worked perfectly. After 7 months, Laura still writes every morning. She's finished two short stories and is almost finished with another. The process is no longer a struggle. One simple action led to the next.

You can also use *other people's actions* as events to remind you of your own. For example:

+ As soon as my husband walks in the door, I'll stop what I'm doing and give him a hug.
+ When my son asks me to do something for him, I'll say, "Let's talk about that after dinner."

Linking to Feelings

You can also link your new action to a *feeling*. This is the exception to the principle of linking to specific actions. It takes a little more attention and awareness to build new habits this way, but the results are worth it. Through this process, you can learn to change your response to circumstances or other people.

Many times, of course, your feelings are a reasonable and appropriate response to your situation. Sometimes, though, certain moods and states of mind become habitual. You feel annoyed with your co-workers, even when they're doing their job. You want to study, but every time you sit down to do it you feel bored.

To link your simple action to a feeling, first identify a particular mood or state of mind you want to shift. For example, you might feel bored, lonely, stressed out, frustrated, lethargic, or worried. Once you've selected the feeling, choose a simple action that is likely to shift that mood. Some common mood-shifting actions are:

+ Listening to music
+ Changing your posture
+ Writing about your feelings
+ Watching something funny
+ Doing a minute of aerobics
+ Taking a few deep breaths

Now make a point of *linking* these as you go through your day. Your simple actions will look something like this:

+ When I notice myself feeling stressed, I'll listen to some light jazz.
+ When I feel worried, I'll watch something funny.
+ When I feel lonely, I'll write for 3 minutes.

You'll need to experiment to see which simple actions make a small but noticeable difference in your mood. Once you discover them, you'll be able to make long-term shifts in how you feel.

Linking to Other Simple Actions

You can also link your new action to *another simple action*. It looks something like this:

+ After I listen to my favorite radio station for 5 minutes, I'll write down three things for which I am grateful.

+ After I hug my daughter, I'll ask about her day.

+ After I take three slow breaths, I'll say something positive.

It's best to start with just one or two simple actions. Over time, as each new action is incorporated into your routine, you can add more. That's how you build *routines*. For example, your morning routine might look something like this:

+ When my alarm rings, I'll get out of bed.

+ As soon as I get up, I'll step into the shower.

+ When I finish my shower, I'll wake up the kids.

+ After they get up, I'll give them a hug.

And so on. If you feel frazzled in the mornings, or find yourself rushing to get places on time, a routine helps reduce stress and provide order.

Exercise 8.1

What regular consistent action can you take to move yourself toward your goal? How will you anchor that action in time? How might you link it to:

+ *A time or a place?*   + *A feeling?*

+ *An event?*   + *Another simple action?*

Environment

Some environments can sabotage your efforts to change, while others can make the new action seem almost natural. If you've ever watched kids rolling down a grassy hill, you'll know that they don't need to force themselves. They just lie down at the top of the hill, hold their arms close to their sides, and let gravity take over. The steep hill makes their hillside roll simply happen. If you plan your environment well, you'll notice a shift in your ability to get things done. You'll more easily move through the actions you need to take to finish your task.

Your environment is made up of:

1. The appropriate tools and supplies you need

2. The right people

Again, let's look at the factors one at a time.

Gathering Tools & Supplies

For our purposes, let's say that your consistent action will happen in a particular place. For Tonya and Lauren, it was at their desk. For Janae, it was in the family room. It could be the kitchen table or the front porch steps – anywhere, as long as it's a place you can easily make a part of your routine.

Once you find that space, having the right tools and supplies at hand is essential. Otherwise, there's a good chance you'll find yourself distracted before you even start. If the first 5 minutes of your writing time is spent looking through your drawers for paper, it's not hard to notice that those drawers really need organizing. If your search for your exercise clothes means looking through the dryer, you might decide that now is a good time to fold the laundry.

When you're creating a new habit, taking a few extra minutes to look for a phone number or printer paper or your yoga mat is enough to derail the process. You can prevent these distractions by setting up your workspace (or kitchen or exercise space) *in advance.*

Make sure that everything you need is ready to go. When Alexi made a commitment to make 40 phone calls a day, she made it as easy as possible for herself to jump right in. She printed out her next day's list of contacts and phone numbers the afternoon before.

If you're writing a resume, you'll probably want a cleared-off desk and a computer. If you're sketching, you'll want a sketch pad and pencils ready to go. For putting together a budget, you'll need your data – plus a spreadsheet or paper, a pencil, and a calculator. You get the idea.

Preventing Distractions

For most people, there are dozens of surprises – big and small – that come up every day. Some of them are unavoidable. Someone asks you for a favor. Your colleague calls in sick. A deadline is moved up. You don't have the resources that you need to get something done. These are real events that you must deal with, and that takes up the time you were counting on for your new habits.

When something unexpected happens, it throws you off your entire routine, and it takes a lot of energy to get back on track. Distractions can undermine new habits, so it's important to have a plan to respond.

Miles, a college student, had a big test coming up, but he put off studying. His problem was one of *preventable distractions.* He'd be studying, and an email would pop into his in-box. His cell phone would beep. A friend would drop by. The constant interruptions made it hard for him to study.

Emails, phone calls, and friends mean a chance to connect, and they are therefore hard to ignore. Once a new email enters your awareness or your phone is chiming, the impulse to respond becomes almost irresistible. The best way to get things done is to plan your "connection time" in advance.

For Miles, that time was scheduled for the afternoon. This meant that in the mornings, he closed his browser, turned off his phone, and shut the door to his dorm room when he was studying. These things were difficult to do at first. However, once Miles did them, his study habits and grades improved. In the last two months of the semester, he raised his grades in almost every class.

Removing temptation works well for preventable distractions. Benjamin – who was trying to significantly reduce his online time – packed up his high-powered gaming computer and started using one that was much more basic. Of course, he could have pulled out the fancy computer anytime, but the extra 10 minutes it took was enough to help him stay on track with his new resolution. He cut down his gaming time from over 3 hours a day to almost none.

There's another kind of preventable distraction that may feel very familiar to you. It's the kind that comes from last-minute projects or surprise deadlines. For example, you suddenly remember that you have a Board Meeting tomorrow, and you need to prepare. Your 8-year-old son reminds you that Halloween is Saturday night, and he needs a costume. Your daughter's science fair project is due in 2 days.

Real emergencies are things like a broken water heater or a virus that puts you in bed. For most people, though, real emergencies are few and far between. Most last-minute surprises come from gaps in planning, and they are in fact preventable.

There are many ways to approach this kind of distraction. One is to plan time each day or each week to handle the unexpected. That way, you can still finish the projects you've planned (for more on this, see Chapter 6, "Plan"). Another is to make sure that every event gets on your calendar – your Board Meetings, the science fair, the Halloween party. Then, as you look through your week, you can plan around these events and schedule the preparation time you need. A third way, and perhaps the most effective, is when you agree to something new, make sure you really have time for it. We'll talk more about this in Chapter 9 ("Flow"). In each case, arranging your environment can help you eliminate preventable distractions.

Asking for What You Need

There's an African proverb that says, "If you want to go fast, go alone. If you want to go far, go together."

Asking for what you need can enable you to go farther. Whatever you're looking for – more money, better communication, more time with your partner – asking is a simple and effective way to help you get there.

It couldn't get simpler. In spite of that, many people don't do it. They're worried about creating obligations or inconvenience or being rejected. According to Linda Babcock and Sara Laschever – who teach negotiation skills to business students, people often don't ask for things that matter to them. Because of this, folks lose out on hundreds of thousands of dollars of lifetime earnings, as well as more interesting projects, balanced workloads, and greater well-being.[4]

In my experience, people don't ask for a great variety of reasons. Some of these are:

+ **You don't want to seem greedy:** *"She'll think I'm asking for too much."*

+ **You don't want to bother anyone:** *"He's probably too busy."*

+ **You don't want to stir things up:** *"She might be upset if I bring that up."*

+ **It's too big a risk:** *"He's going to say, 'No.' So what's the point?"*

All of these reasons are versions of *fear.*

Asking for something that matters can be difficult. It means taking a stand, stepping onto center stage and into the spotlight. It can be scary to show the world – or even your partner, colleague, or boss – what is deeply important to you.

For many people, fear in one form or another is the main thing that stands in the way of dreams. I don't necessarily mean big, earth-shaking fears. I mean the tiny, moment-to-moment anxious thoughts and worries that come up every day, like the fear of disappointing someone or the fear of being judged. It's easier to stay hidden in the wings than to confront these types of fears.

Pushing yourself to center stage demands integrity. It requires you to be honest with yourself about what really matters, and then speak up about it. Each time you do this, you gain confidence. Eleanor Roosevelt said, "You gain strength, courage, and confidence by every experience in which you really stop to look fear in the face." She goes on to suggest the antidote: "You must do the thing you think you cannot do."

My client Erin decided to challenge herself by creating a habit of asking. For several weeks, she made a point of asking for five things every day, just to build her skill. Some of her requests were small, and others were substantial. The results were amazing. Not only did she end the month feeling more confident, but also she was offered a summer's employment on a project she was excited about.

Consider where the question of "asking" touches your life. On what subject do you need to start admitting what you really want? Your salary? A promotion? A sharing of household responsibility? Time with people you care about? Knowing the truth and taking it to heart can help you stop settling for the way things are. Maybe it's time to rock the boat.

If you don't ask, the answer will always be *no*. If you do ask, however, the results are likely to be positive. It turns out that most people want to be responsive to the needs of others. Asking gives them the opportunity to be generous and feel good about themselves. In your personal life, asking can reduce stress, improve communication, and better negotiate shared responsibilities.

Exercise 8.2

a. How will you structure your environment to support your action?

b. What emergencies can you predict?

c. Who could you talk to about something that you need?

Changing Habits You *Don't* Want

There's another way to increase the chances you'll follow through, and that is by focusing on what you don't want. You can do this in a couple of ways: you can make the undesirable behavior hard, or you can focus on the consequence of not making the change.

Alexi chose the first way. She wanted to stop working in the evening, so she left her work and her laptop at the office. Working at home was now hard, because she didn't have access to most of the things she needed. One of my clients stopped smoking by first limiting her access to cigarettes. She bought only one pack at a time, and kept them separate from her other purchases. Because of this, she had to make a 20-minute trip to the store for each new pack. Later she used other strategies to stop altogether.

The second way works well for problems with strong negative consequences, like an urgent health concern or a problem with addiction. In situations like this, either the pull of the old behavior is very strong, or there's no time to take small steps to nudge yourself into a new lifestyle. The change needs to happen right away, and it needs to stick. When this happens, you need to up the ante.

One way is to do this is to create a goal compelling enough to pull you – or *scare you* – into making it happen. This strategy is sometimes referred to as making a "Ulysses Contract."

Ulysses was the King of Ithaca, hero of Homer's epic poem *Odyssey*. The King wanted to hear the famous song of the Sirens on his way home after the Trojan War. But Ulysses knew that if he did, he wouldn't be able to resist their call. A song of such beauty would lead him to change course and be dashed to death on the rocks, as others had been before him.

So he made a deal. Ulysses asked his crew to bind him to the mast of their ship and plug their own ears until they were well past the danger. When they were once again on their path home and he could again think rationally, his crew could untie his ropes and release the King.

In essence, Ulysses made a deal in the present to motivate himself to do the right thing in the future, when it really mattered.

How do you up the ante?

A *Ulysses Contract* is an agreement that has two features:

+ It's easy to commit to in the present.

+ It provides an incentive for the future that gives you the emotional energy to resist the pull of old habits.

The only requirement is that the incentive be compelling. It can be a reward that you enjoy and is good for you, or something you very much don't want to happen. A typical example is giving a significant amount of money – let's say $500 – to a friend. If you stick to your exercise program or you stay away from cigarettes, you get it back in a month. If you don't, your friend keeps it – or worse, the money is given to a cause you detest.

Once the contract is made, the energy needed for your commitment becomes less than the energy needed to fall off course. Change becomes the path of least resistance.

Exercise 8.3

. . . .

What is likely to distract you from your new action? How can you remove that temptation, or discourage yourself from responding to it?

. . . .

You now know how to use consistent action to create habits, and how to create a supportive environment to keep yourself moving forward. You can also use the tools in Chapter 7, "Shrink," to increase your motivation by making the task even smaller, and therefore easier.

Once you're taking small, regular actions, you'll be well on your way to accomplishing your goals. Your habits and routines are still new, however, and new challenges can dislodge them. In the next chapter "Flow," we'll look at some of the most common obstacles to change and how to handle them.

Key Points

- ✦ The key to lasting change is turning your small actions into habits.

- ✦ New habits are built by linking them to a specific time and place, an event, a feeling, or to another small action. A series of small actions helps you build *routines*.

- ✦ With the right environment, you don't need to rely on willpower.

- ✦ If change is urgent, you can up the ante to bring about the change you want.

Simple Actions

- ✦ Choose something you'd like to do, and craft it as a compelling goal.

- ✦ Make a small change in your environment to support your goal. If you want to write a memo, put your notes next to your computer. If you need to set up a meeting, get the phone numbers ready. If your goal is to start running, place your running shoes by the front door.

- ✦ Do *something*: write a sentence, make one call, or run around the block.

- ✦ Increase your staying power by keeping your actions small.

- ✦ Choose a goal you know is important, and write a brief but powerful Ulysses Contract to provide incentive.

Chapter 9

Flow

*"Obstacles don't have to stop you.
If you run into a wall, don't turn around and give up.
Figure out how to climb it, go through it, or work around it."*

– Michael Jordan

***Flow* is the ability** to move forward steadily and continuously, like water through a riverbed. A river sweeps past rocks and flows around logs, changing course as little as possible as it continues to its destination. The analogy is apt: people can accomplish difficult things when they navigate around obstacles in their path and keep moving toward a goal.

No matter how thoughtfully you imagine, plan, and act, obstacles will come up. We usually think of obstacles as *outside* of us, and it's easy to think of events that present major challenges. Circumstances can be difficult, but many of the real battles are *within ourselves*. Too often, we undermine ourselves by the way we *interpret* events.

In this chapter, we'll consider several strategies that can help you overcome internal obstacles. Each of these will make it far easier to navigate the external obstacles you encounter, and also make it far more likely that you'll reach your goal.

Strategy 1: Change the Way You View Failure

Failure isn't an endpoint. It's a turning point.

All of us fail, all the time. Toddlers learning to walk fail more often than they manage to stand. Kids learning to read make thousands of "mistakes" before getting the gist of a story.

Athletes fail all the time. Michael Jordan said, "I've missed more than 9,000 shots in my career. I've lost almost 300 games. Twenty-six times, I've been trusted to take the game's winning shot and missed. I've failed over and over and over again in my life. And that is why I succeed."[1] The world of business also has its share of failure. In fact, Thomas J. Watson, founder of IBM, had this to say on the subject: "The formula for success is quite simple: double your rate of failure."

Failure is not unusual when you're aiming high. Vera Wang didn't make the U.S. Olympic figure skating team, so she changed course and entered the field of fashion. Now she is one of the most respected designers in the world. Steven Spielberg applied twice to get into the University of Southern California's (USC's) School of Cinema Arts. He was rejected both times. Abraham Lincoln lost eight elections before becoming U.S. President (his third political win). Vincent van Gogh painted over 900 paintings in his lifetime. He sold only one.

Athletes alternate successes with injuries and setbacks, and many never meet their most ambitious goals. Programmers, artists, athletes, and entrepreneurs keep trying – not because they succeed most of the time – but because they love what they do.

The biggest problem with labeling an effort a failure is thinking of failure as a problem in the first place. Failure is, in fact, an excellent way to learn. When you take on something difficult, it's likely that you'll encounter some obstacles – maybe big ones. You may not make it past them on the first try. Perhaps a better word for failure would be an "experiment."

Indeed, failure is inevitable when you're experimenting with new and different approaches. Plus, side paths and diversions are part of the very road we travel when innovating. These developments are a problem only when they lead to inaction, when because of them you stop moving forward.

There are many possible ways to work around obstacles, to succeed where you have failed before, to move forward in the face of other peoples' comments or your own worry and doubt. Below is an exercise that will remind you that you too have failed, yet still continued to forge on toward success – probably many times.

Exercise 9.1

Think of one or two things that you've accomplished in your life that you're proud of. What did it take to accomplish them? Do you attribute your success to luck or perseverance? Did you want to throw up your hands in frustration at any point? What are some of the ways you found to work around the problems you encountered?

Strategy 2: Fall in Love with the Process

Focusing on the success or failure of a goal can easily lead to inaction. To avoid doing something wrong, you don't do *anything*. You say no to an invitation, turn down the promotion, walk away from a chance to perform. No matter how much you've been looking for the opportunity, you just don't feel "ready."

The problem in such cases may be an over-focus on your goal. Yes, it's important and inspiring to envision success. And it's an essential early step in accomplishing a difficult task. However, a future-focus can sometimes get in the way of moving forward. Sometimes it's better to focus on the present, on one step at a time. Forget the result, at least for now.

Practice and process are key to keeping you on track. If you want to become a concert pianist, imagining a key performance might inspire you, but it's even more important to love the practice. To accomplish great things, Gandhi said, "Satisfaction lies in the effort."

Mikaela Shiffrin, the 2014 gold medalist in women's slalom skiing, said that a big factor in her success was that her parents helped her focus on athletic skill rather than on winning or losing. In the final races, she focused on the process instead of the results. "I kept thinking that I had to keep my skis moving downhill," she said.

Similarly, to end up with a good result, it's important to enjoy the learning, the practice, and the problem-solving. It's fun to win, but in the long run it's more important to find joy in being a better skier, marriage partner, or decision-maker.

As discussed in the last section, problems are part of any worthy endeavor. You'll do your best to solve the problems that come up, but it won't always be clear how to find the best solution – or even if there *is* a solution.

Some common responses make this process harder. You might feel frustrated or anxious about your ability to find the "right" solution. You might get stuck, and waste valuable energy feeling resentful, looking for someone to blame, or blaming yourself.

Fortunately, as humans, we're excellent problem-solvers. When confronted with something difficult, there's a natural urge to figure it out and a moment of satisfaction in the "ah hah!" moment when we see something from a different perspective. Focusing on your natural ability to solve problems, and the burst of clarity that results, is satisfying and can keep you moving forward.

If you're a writer, love the process of putting words on paper. If you're a swimmer, swim for the feeling of your body in motion. If an obstacle comes up or you make a mistake, enjoy the problem-solving. With this approach, you'll find that there's a good chance you'll reach your goal faster than when you are mainly attached to "doing everything right."

Exercise 9.2

What do you need to get better at so you can reach your goal? What can you find to love about this process of improving and learning?

Strategy 3: Keep Track of Your Wrong Guesses

It's fun to tell people when you finally get hired, get engaged, or lose 37 pounds. However, the path to accomplishing those things likely included a process of experimentation and wrong guesses, and you'd be in good company if you didn't advertise those (failing) experiences. Few people talk about their mistakes.

There are many reasons that we keep quiet. For some, the culprit is perfectionism, the myth that we're supposed to have everything figured out before presenting it to the outside world. In addition, it can be daunting to try new things publicly. We fear the embarrassment and perhaps shame of a mis-step. Because we're so averse to failure, people tend to sweep failed efforts under the rug – to get rid of the evidence, so to speak. Some work situations encourage this behavior by discouraging wrong guesses or punishing "poor performance." After all, you're paid to succeed, right? And if you work at home as an entrepreneur or parent, who wants to feel like a struggling business owner or less than perfect parent?

However, what doesn't work is just as important as what does. If you don't pay attention to your mistakes, you're likely to repeat them. If you don't talk about mis-steps, it could take longer to achieve your goal. You miss the opportunity to develop a realistic picture of what it really takes to tackle challenges.

With this kind of behavior, we're creating a mythology around success. When there's a culture of hiding mistakes, it gives the impression that the people who do succeed are especially talented or smart, and somehow different from those of us who struggle.

Realistically, all learning is based on trial and error. You didn't wait for perfect balance before you started riding a bike. You hopped on the bike, wobbled, fell down, got up and tried again. There was no way to skip the wobbling – each wobble taught you something about balance. Wrong guesses helped you learn.

Real failures don't come from mistakes. They come from not trying.

Instead of avoiding mistakes, consider seeking them out. Thomas Edison made this remark about inventing the light bulb: "I have not failed. I've just found 10,000 ways that won't work." Imagine what Edison must have learned from those wrong guesses. Imagine what *you* could learn.

Consider, for example, how well you could perform in a job interview if you knew what interviewers look for and what they shun. Imagine how quickly you might improve a business proposal or a presentation if you got regular feedback on what worked well and what didn't.

My client Tonya, the one applying for social service jobs, understood what she wanted because she'd already worked in organizations that were driven by the bottom line. Those prior job experiences weren't failures, because they provided her with information – background that eventually helped her find work she preferred and loved.

In reality, there's no clear dividing line between success and failure. There's only learning along the way.

Strategy 4: Change Your Story

Stories are powerful. The stories you tell yourself affect not only whether or not you reach your goal, but also how difficult you'll find your path. Often the biggest obstacles are the insurmountable walls of our own stories.

When my daughter Julia was about five, our family had a ritual. When something went wrong, when she was feeling disappointed or frustrated, we would do our best to offer comfort. Sometimes it was easy – all it took was a hug or a story. At other times, calming her felt impossible. Her frustration would trigger our frustration, which would further trigger hers – resulting in a kind of spiraling "cycle of frustration." *Distracting* didn't work. *Ignoring* made it worse.

We found that stories born out of that frustration raised these beliefs: "She's doing it on purpose." "She doesn't want to be comforted." "She's mad at us." "She needs a time-out." These beliefs tended to lead to more frustration.

As parents, we needed a story that would take us out of the problem, even if we didn't fully understand its cause. The new story was simpler. Our daughter was crying, and we wanted to help her get back to calm. That more practical "story" led us to try something new. My husband and I started a ritual, where we walked through our backyard with our daughter, looking for smiles.

Smiles can be elusive, especially when you're frustrated, so sometimes the search took a while. We'd look behind bushes and under rocks. We'd walk up a hill to the very top of our yard and look along the fence behind the vines of bougainvillea. Sometimes we'd pick an orange and eat it while we thought about where to look next. The amazing thing was that we always found a smile eventually!

What we really found was a new way to *see* the problem. What had been frustration became a journey, one that led us to smiles.

Martin Rossman, M.D., describes how the images we create can change our mood and overcome obstacles. He suggests that by creating healing imagery, we can create changes in both body and mind. As he suggests, stories and images actually change the neural pathways in our brain.[2] As a matter of fact, researchers have found evidence of increased neural connectivity in the brain when someone learns another person's story.[3]

Neuroscientist Gregory S. Berns led a study at Emory University designed to look at how stories affect the brain. Over a period of 9 days, twenty-one undergraduates read the fast-paced novel *Pompeii*. Berns' team used functional MRI scans to measure activity in specific brain regions before participants started the novel, during the 9 days of reading, and for 5 days after the novel was finished. They found that the act of reading the novel created changes in the brain's neural pathways, and that those changes persisted through the days after the students finished reading. Novels, we know, can affect our thoughts and mood. Berns suggests that they might also affect our biology.[4]

Good stories lead to action, while negative ones can keep you stuck. When I first met Sandra, she wasn't doing the design work she had trained for. Her story was this: "Our business needs administrative help so that's what I need to do. Besides, the economy is bad. It's not a good time to set out on my own. People won't want to pay enough for my work." Her story had a point – building a new business *is* difficult. However, with that story in mind, her inevitable conclusion was to give up... or at least wait out the economy.

Later on, Sandra and I talked about another possible story: "My time and energy has gone into our joint business so far, for good reason. But now it's time to spend some of my work time doing what I enjoy. I can start small. Here's what I might do to find just one job..."

Changing your story can change the outcome. For instance, a story of "I'll never get this right" depletes your energy and holds you back. One of my clients, Ryan, had a story that he would always be afraid to fly. He traveled rarely, giving up chances to visit family and advance at work. When Ryan adopted a different story – one of "I have the power to change my thoughts" or "This is tough but I'm learning to do something new" – he felt energized.

Most often, it's not the obstacle itself that's holding you up – the missed job opportunity, the cranky six-year-old, the water-leak damage.

Those are difficult problems, to be sure. What really gets in the way, though, is how you *think* about those problems – whether your thoughts *paralyze or motivate*. Changing the story changes *your response*, which in turn changes the result and either holds you back or moves you to action.

Exercise 9.3

....

Think of a time when you were really frustrated – when something you were trying to do wasn't working. How did you explain that to yourself? Is there a more positive or helpful way of looking at the same series of events?

....

Strategy 5: Don't Believe Everything You Think

Thoughts shape feelings and behaviors, so it's important to choose them carefully. If your mood is low, there's a good chance that inaccurate or distorted thoughts create a feeling that something is wrong. One way of categorizing thoughts that cause problems is to divide them into thoughts about the past, present, and future.

Thoughts about the Past

Tens of thousands of thoughts go through your mind every day. These thoughts can be positive, neutral, or negative, and of course, it's the negative ones that cause us trouble. Negative thoughts about the past can be replays of situations that didn't go well. These look something like this:

+ I can't believe I couldn't answer that question... the interviewer probably thought I'd never done a budget before.

+ I bet I looked pretty stupid. They probably thought I was a complete beginner.

+ Here's what I should have said...

It's one thing for thoughts like these to cross your mind, and another if you start to see them as the truth. By entertaining their veracity, you can start to feel guilty, embarrassed, angry, anxious, or depressed.

There are several ways to change the impact of negative perceptions. The first step is to *simply notice them*. You'll probably be surprised at how often thoughts like this drift through your mind. Learning to be aware of them is a key step in changing how you think, and sometimes this act alone is enough to take away their charge. It's a key part of mindfulness (see Chapter 4, "Pause").

Once you're aware of them, notice how the thoughts naturally come and go. As you move through your day, they're replaced by different thoughts with a different emotional tone. Notice those thoughts too and recognize them for what they are: *just thoughts*. Enjoy the emotional distance this process creates.

Thoughts about the Present

Much negative thinking comes from evaluating what you're doing while you're doing it. Some types of present-oriented thinking are *always/ never thinking*, *I'm not okay/You're not okay*, and *"shoulds."*

Always/Never thinking distorts reality in a way that makes change seem impossible.

+ I always mess up interviews.

+ "You never help with dinner."

This kind of thinking paints you into a corner. When you think in absolutes (like with the thought above about interviews), it's hard to see possibilities. When you're talking with someone else, it's a great way to get the conversation off track. Let's take the comment "You never help with dinner," for example. Instead of successfully recruiting help with dinner, you're likely to trigger defensiveness. The person you're talking to objects to the "never," and the two of you end up arguing about how many times last week she really helped.

I'm not okay/You're not okay thinking is loaded with criticism and blame.

- ✦ I'm not okay: Why did I let her talk me into playing softball? I suck at it.

- ✦ You're not okay: "If you had listened to me, everything would be fine!"

For "I'm not okay" thoughts, an *assertive response* often helps: "It's true that I didn't hit the ball, but I haven't played softball in years. Besides, this is a kick-back league, and I'm doing it for fun, so who cares if I hit the ball every time I'm up?"

"You're not okay" thoughts avoid responsibility and encourage bad feelings, but we're often tempted to take them seriously. Why? Well, we like to find solutions to problems, and identifying the culprit *feels* like a solution. Moreover, blaming has the added benefit of letting ourselves off the hook. To avoid making "you're not okay" statements, *ownership* is key: "I'll make sure I'm here on time from now on."

If you have an issue with someone else's behavior, you can address that in a separate, *non-blaming* conversation where you ask for corrective action: "I'd like everyone here by 8:30 every morning. Please do whatever you need to do to be here on time. Thanks."

Shoulds

- ✦ I should go to that meeting.

- ✦ I should study more.

- ✦ I should exercise every morning.

The biggest problem with "shoulds" is that they *undermine motivation* by piling on anxiety, guilt, and sometimes shame. Those emotions more often lead to inaction rather than action.

The accompanying thoughts are critical, not inspiring, because they focus on your "bad" behavior, not the solution, the benefits, or the consequences of a particular behavior. The thoughts sidestep your own feelings and wishes, and they present the issue as if an outside authority were demanding it.

Alexi, for example, believed that she "should" be available at all times to her interns. As a result, they stopped by randomly to ask questions and share their thoughts. However, her "drop in" policy was undermining the work she (and they) actually needed to get done.

"Have you thought about office hours?" I asked. Alexi had not, and she was concerned that the interns wouldn't be able to do their work without her immediate advice. Besides, Alexi was proud of her ability to be responsive. Nonetheless, if she wanted her evenings back, this pattern was going to have to change.

Setting office hours worked. Her interns took the change in stride, and they started to do their own research instead of immediately turning to Alexi. So not only did Alexi create solid blocks of time in which she could work without interruption, but she also inadvertently helped her interns become more proactive and independent. Because they had to wait, the interns had more time to organize their thoughts, and their remaining requests were more fully developed.

Alexi mentally challenged her "should" and made a change. Another approach is to substitute "want" or "could," and then add an explanation. The new wording avoids the feeling of parental authority, and instead it conveys the benefit of the new behavior.

+ I *want to* study more so I'll really understand this material. I'll need this background in my new position.

+ I *could* exercise every morning. I have time then, and walking or yoga would give me more energy at the start of my day. I could try it for a week and see if I like it.

Another way to combat "shoulds" is by creating *an "if... then" statement*. This is another way to state the benefit.

- *If* I go to that meeting, *then* I'll be able to present my new idea.
- *If* I don't go to that meeting, *then* I'll lose the opportunity to vote on our next project.

Thoughts about the Future

Cory, like many people, worried about the future. Worry often comes in the form of *"what if"* questions:

- *What if* I lose my job?
- *What if* I can't think of anything to say?
- *What if* someone doesn't *like* what I say?

Future outcomes are always uncertain, and "what if" questions play into this. One way to lessen the power of these questions is to challenge them. Create an *assertive response* that acknowledges the small bit of truth embedded in the concern, but restates the consequence and the implications. Cory did it this way:

- It's true that I can't always think of something to say when I'm in a group. But I'm learning, and I can see that I'm getting better at it every week.

Another way is to create *a detailed plan*. The first general step in a plan might look something like this:

- If I lose my job, I'll call five people I know that might have leads about new jobs. I'll follow up on those leads, and I'll check online resources for opportunities.

Strategy 6: Assume There *Is* a Solution

You can sometimes find an unexpected answer, a spark of inspiration, or an upside-down way of solving a problem. When you feel stuck, anything that you haven't tried before has promise. To do this, you'll need *creativity, persistence,* and some *comfort with ambiguity and confusion.*

Creativity

Creativity is something we all need, every day. We need the ability to step out of our routines and break the rules. Ultimately, there is no rule for the best way to break the rules. Inspired ideas can come from spending time alone and from brainstorming with other people, from working within a structure and from "thinking outside the box."

In a 2010 survey conducted by IBM, 1500 CEOs from 60 countries were interviewed in-person over several months. The CEOs identified creativity as the *most important quality* in prospective employees. These executives viewed creativity as an essential ingredient in a world that is growing in complexity and interconnectedness, and they ranked it above such characteristics as vision, discipline, and integrity.[5]

Rob used a creative approach for job interviews. Having been out of work for almost a year, he was feeling discouraged about his chances of finding something promising in his field. When the ideal job happened to come along, I helped Rob land it by using *storytelling* as part of his interview. We crafted compelling stories about his clients that highlighted his strengths, and he sprinkled them throughout his winning interview.

Persistence

In addition to creativity, you'll need *persistence*. Sometimes you'll need to try dozens, even hundreds of solutions before you find one that works. Persistence is part of what got the Apollo 13 astronauts safely home.

There are few things as well planned as a space mission. In spite of that, the Apollo 13 mission in 1970 almost led to disaster. After some routine procedures were completed, a spark from an exposed wire in the ship's oxygen tank caused an explosion that disabled much of the vessel's equipment. The astronauts were 200,000 miles away from Earth at the time.

From the ground, flight director Gene Kranz led thousands of engineers and flight controllers as they worked round the clock to develop new procedures.[6] The astronauts remained confident[7] as they tried one plan after another, all the while living in a capsule designed to keep them alive for 45 hours, when they needed 90 to safely return to Earth.[8] There was always something else to try. It was both creativity and persistence that kept the astronauts and ground crew from giving up. On April 17, 1970, after several challenging days, the spacecraft successfully splashed down in the Pacific Ocean with all three astronauts surviving.

Comfort with Confusion

Confusion is a natural part of learning. Before you can come up with solutions that work, you'll need to get comfortable with confusion, wrong guesses, and ambiguity. Your first ideas are most likely your "go to" answers. To expand your repertoire of ideas, allow the confusion and keep going. Let yourself experience the discomfort, the tension of ambiguity. Don't be in a hurry to get through it. Learn to tolerate the muddle.

The path to your goal will rarely be as straight and smooth as you imagine. It's important to accept the risk – and the inevitability – that things will go wrong. Again, assume that there *is* a solution, and proceed from there.

When you're comfortable with moving through obstacles, there will be no stopping you. You'll be ready to celebrate your achievements. Celebration, however, is not just about the big event at the end of all the work you've done. It's also about each step along the way, the tiny successes and failures that got you there. The next chapter shows why celebration is essential for creating change, and it offers some novel ways to celebrate even the smallest accomplishments.

Key Points

+ Failure is a great way to learn.
+ Instead of "failure," think "experiment."

+ Fall in love with the process, instead of the result.

+ Keep track of your wrong guesses. Knowing what doesn't work saves a lot of time.

+ Changing your story can change the outcome.

+ Don't believe everything you think.

Simple Actions that Build Confidence

+ Change your body language.

+ Step out of your comfort zone.

+ Prepare questions in advance.

+ Do some research.

+ Rehearse, as if you were going to perform (even if you're not).

+ Reflect on your strengths.

Simple Actions to Overcome Obstacles

+ **Pause.** Take a moment, an hour, a day away from the problem you want to solve, and allow yourself to reflect. Provide time for creating a mental space for new ideas to emerge. (See Chapter 4.)

+ **Daydream.** We seek to make connections between things that at first don't seem to go together. Allow your mind to sift through your experience, looking for something new and unusual that might shed light on a problem.

+ **Be willing to be bored, or boring.** For a specific amount of time, try to sit with the feeling of restlessness and the thought that there's nothing new to ponder. "Be with" your boredom.

+ **Create alternatives.** Don't go for a solution right away. The first things that occur to you are likely to be your "standard" solutions – the ones that occur to you all the time. For a new perspective, generate 10 solutions, or perhaps a hundred, before stopping to consider which one is best.

✦ **Look for the seeds of potential in *every* idea.** The most "ridiculous" possibility might contain the seeds of an innovative idea or experiment. Find something useful in every idea before tossing it. If you're working with others, encourage wacky ideas and off-beat perceptions. The craziest idea might turn out to be the most useful.

✦ **Encourage a meditative state.** The state between wakefulness and sleep, a *hypnogogic state*, is conducive to innovation. It can come about through meditation, hypnosis, a particular type of biofeedback referred to as Alpha-Theta Neurofeedback, or by simply allowing yourself to drift toward sleep without falling asleep. In this state, thought processes change and boundaries relax. Great thinkers, such as Thomas Edison and Friedrich August Kekulé (a chemist who figured out the shape of a molecule called benzene), have induced a hypnogogic state to enhance their own creativity.

✦ **Find a metaphor.** I sometimes ask my clients to find a metaphor for their problem or conflict. Some people have imagined their difficulty as a "road closed" sign, a boulder, or strange creatures. Couples have labeled their problem communication The Dark Desert, The Hurricane, and The Saboteur.

✦ **Ask yourself what a trusted mentor might advise.** Your mentor can be a living person, or an imaginary character from history or fiction.

✦ **Use art.** Doodle, draw, paint, sketch. Keep your hand moving as ideas come to you.

✦ **Tap into your dreams.** Think of a dream you had recently, or long ago. How can that dream be a metaphor for the problem you're trying to solve?

+ **Collaborate.** Brainstorming with a group can generate many new ideas quickly. One women's group uses this strategy specifically to generate new ideas to help members with work, relationships, and personal problems. Each month about 30 women gather. One member takes notes while others brainstorm on a specific, targeted question. The person who asked the question leaves the meeting with dozens of new ideas.

Chapter 10

Celebrate

*"The more you praise and celebrate your life,
the more there is to celebrate."*

– Oprah Winfrey

Congratulations, you did it! By now you've accomplished something, and you deserve to celebrate. Pat yourself on the back, call a friend to brag, or take yourself out to dinner. Celebration is a key part of change.

If you find yourself thinking, "All I did was write a paragraph" or "What's the big deal about walking to work *one day,*" know that paragraphs and walks are worthy accomplishments. Celebrations aren't just for big events and for children's birthdays. They're for everyone, anytime you meet a goal. By savoring what you've done, recognizing what you've accomplished, and acknowledging yourself as an agent of change, you help make change visible and lasting.

Celebration is a key part of change. It helps build self-respect, provides energy, and serves as a reminder that you have helped create something positive in your life and in the world. It's an antidote to feeling like you have "nothing to show" for your efforts. Celebration provides the burst of excitement you need to keep going.

Small Celebrations

Celebrations can be big or small. "Celebration" here includes everything from public gatherings to private moments of self-acknowledgement. It is a reward for anything you complete.

Small celebrations can fit into the tiniest corners of your life. If you have time to take a breath or stretch your legs, you have time to celebrate. Sure, big achievements – like landing a fabulous job or opening your new business – deserve a big celebration, maybe an open house, a dinner out, or a weekend away. Smaller accomplishments warrant smaller celebrations. Give yourself a hug, play a bit of your favorite song, do a jumping jack of exuberance, or simply tell yourself, "Good job!" Small gestures like these can take less than a minute, yet pack a big punch. They make you happy.

According to Daniel Gilbert, Harvard professor and the author of *Stumbling on Happiness*, feeling happy isn't about big things. Rather, it's about hundreds of little things. In a 2012 interview with the *Harvard Business Review*, he said, "The *frequency* of your positive experiences is a much better predictor of your happiness than is the *intensity* of your positive experiences... How good your experiences are doesn't matter nearly as much as how many good experiences you have."[1]

A moment of celebration can help you remember that big accomplishments are built on hundreds of tiny ones. Winning a game of *Monopoly* isn't just about the last move you made – it's about *all* the moves you made along the way. Reaching the pinnacle of Mt. Everest starts long before you take the first step, with many small decisions and plans, and the building of networks. It's important to notice these. Cultivate positive experiences by adding small moments of self-appreciation and fun into each day.

When celebrations are small, you can have them often. Give yourself the gift of a small celebration every time you:

- ✦ Make an important decision.
- ✦ Complete a task.
- ✦ Reach a milestone.

As you begin to do this, notice how your mood, energy, and productivity increase.

Exercise 10.1
. . . .

a. *When in your day could you recognize a small success?*

b. *How would you like to celebrate your accomplishment?*
Choose a tiny celebration from the list at the end of this chapter,
or create one of your own.

. . . .

Change Builds on Change

"Celebrate what you want to see more of," says Tom Peters, author of *In Search of Excellence*. When you consciously *focus* on what you have accomplished by celebrating, you increase the chances that it will happen again. This isn't magic. When you're focused, you'll notice things you otherwise might have missed, like a snippet of conversation or a reference to someone you'd like to meet. Your increased focus will also help you ignore things that might normally distract you and slow you down.

Celebrating helps small change snowball into bigger, more far-reaching change. You'll remember how this happened for Sandra. She started with a simple daily walk. She celebrated these walks with a brief word of self-appreciation. "Good for me," she said to herself. "I'm taking action."

The positive words helped her persevere during the first difficult weeks when her efforts didn't seem to be working. Her tiny celebrations helped her continue anyway, which in turn led to weekend hikes and backpacking trips with her husband. As she and Jay celebrated their new healthier lifestyle, they recognized their common goal of excellent health.

As they celebrated their increasing fitness, Sandra and Jay found it natural to also want to eat well. They worked on this together. In addition, by adding small touches to meals and working hard to keep the conversation light, Sandra helped make family meals a kind of celebration too. Over time, this was enough to shift family conversations from tense to enjoyable.

For Cory, as well, change built upon change. As he learned to manage stress, Cory got to be comfortable around the people he worked with. Tiny celebrations helped build his confidence, and he started to notice that his skill in handling conflict was growing. His small accomplishments and positive outlook were seen by management as signs of leadership, and he was eventually offered a promotion.

For both Cory and Sandra, celebrating helped them see that each step, no matter how mundane, was part of a journey toward something valuable and inspiring. Making their progress visible through small celebrations helped them keep their goals in mind.

Exercise 10.2
. . . .

By noticing and celebrating small actions, you'll feel more easily drawn toward the goal you imagined in Chapter 5. How can you celebrate the progress you're making now, however small, to encourage more of it in the future?

. . . .

Celebration helps change build on change in some very specific ways.

1. Celebration reinforces habits.

2. Celebration encourages progress.

3. Celebration creates happiness.

Let's look at these one at a time.

Celebration Reinforces Habits

A reward is an essential part of any habit. Rewards provide a sense of satisfaction, and because of this, they provide an urge to repeat the behavior. What gives satisfaction varies from one person to another, so you might have to experiment to find what works best for you. For Alexi, checking off an item on her daily list was enough, and the check itself was the reward. For Cory, it was a simple mental "pat on the back" of "Nice going!"

There is a biochemical basis for the sense of satisfaction connected with rewards. Every time you do something with the anticipation of getting a reward, however small, you get a rush of dopamine. Professor Emerita Loretta Breuning calls dopamine one of "the happy chemicals, because of the powerful effect it has on the brain."[2] When dopamine increases in response to something you do, you're more likely to do that thing again in the future. Thus dopamine helps you learn new patterns of behavior and in essence build new habits.

You'll get this dopamine reward when you accomplish big things, of course. But why wait for 7 months until the project is finished, when you can get a reward 10 times a day? Sandra felt a burst of nostalgia and joy every time she looked at her honeymoon photo. She made that tiny action into a routine and a celebration. Each time she and Jay spent positive time together (and each time she ducked an argument), Sandra reinforced the new behavior by pausing to look at the photo.

Celebration Encourages Progress

Athletes and musicians have coaches to give them feedback on their progress. If you don't have a coach by your side, you have to give yourself feedback. Tracking your progress in written form is one way to do that. When the larger goal feels elusive, looking at a series of checkmarks, some dots on a graph, or a list of things you've accomplished can help you evaluate whether the actions you're taking are helping – or whether you need to change course.

Without some kind of acknowledgement or celebration of progress, it's hard to remember how far you've come. Memory is often unreliable. The vivid detail my clients use to describe their situation at the beginning of counseling seems to fade over time. That's a good thing, for the most part. The problem comes when they feel like they're "not getting anywhere."

Without marking and celebrating progress in some way, it can be hard to see. Think about how children grow. If you haven't seen them for a year or so, you might be amazed at how they look when they're a couple of inches taller. But if they're *your* kids and you see them every day, you probably won't notice the small fraction of an inch that they gained last Saturday. The difference is too small. Tracking and celebrating these changes helps make them visible.

I often create weekly problem-rating scales for my clients to help make progress visible. With one of these scales, Cory tracked the number of social interactions he had every day, so he could see the increase over time. A few months into counseling, when Cory said that he wasn't making any progress, I pulled out the chart. The difference on paper was visible, and the chart allowed him to both acknowledge and celebrate it. Because of this, Cory was easily able to see, and appreciate, how far he'd come.

Exercise 10.3

. . . .

a. Choose one of your goals, and decide how you will visibly mark progress toward that goal.

b. Choose a way to celebrate not only milestones, but also tasks on your way to that goal. You'll find ideas at the end of the chapter.

. . . .

Celebration Creates Happiness

The Dalai Lama says that being happy is what we were born to do. Happiness, in this view, is part of the pathway to a successful life. It's not something we should aspire to, or that we'll find "someday" when we've gone through the difficult parts of life. Instead, it's worth building in happiness right now.

Ron Culberson, author of *Do It Well. Make It Fun* agrees. The key to excellence, he argues, is a combination of focused action and playful celebration.[3] The importance of fun is often missed. Meeting a goal, completing a task or even finishing a project often don't seem worthy of taking the time to enjoy your accomplishments. Yet an ability to do this is key to a satisfying and joyful life. As the saying goes, "It's not about the days in your life, but the life in your days."

Small celebrations are a way to bring life into your days. Laughter, in particular, builds relationships, promotes teamwork, and diffuses tension. Research suggests that laughter boosts your immune system, improves mood, and reduces stress. Celebrating with laughter will help speed you along in unexpected ways.

What better way to celebrate than by rewarding yourself with something you enjoy? How about giving yourself time to talk to a friend, have a bite of chocolate, or spend a half-hour soaking in a bubble bath? You can do these things for their own sake, of course, but you can also use them as rewards as you finish small tasks or reach major milestones. The key to choosing rewards is to make them playful, enjoyable, and fun.

Exercise 10.4

a. List five things that feel fun or that make you laugh. Which of these could you use to help celebrate small successes?

b. For the next week, track the things you do that make you happy. Consider increasing this number for the following week.

Personal Time as Celebration

Personal time is perhaps the simplest form of celebration. It means taking a pause from daily activity to shift perspective or replenish energy. It can be as simple as a coffee break, as deep as a meditation practice, or as extensive as a week-long trip on a cruise ship.

However, rest beyond a lunch period can be hard to get during a typical workday – at least in the U.S. According to a recent survey, 55% of workers don't feel they can leave their desks to take a break. Instead, people rush from one project to the next, often multitasking along the way. The reason most often cited: guilt.[4]

It seems to be just as hard to take scheduled vacation time. A Harris poll showed that only about 40% of adults in the U.S. took or were planning to take a vacation in the summer of 2011. Among those who planned time away, only 35% were planning on truly disconnecting – leaving the email, voicemail, and cell phones for when they return.[5]

A 2012 poll by Expedia tackled the question of why taking time off seems so difficult. Twenty-eight percent of the 500 respondents said they can't afford a vacation; 23% were storing up vacation for "later"; 21% said they couldn't coordinate with other people's schedules; and 24% either traded their vacation time for more money or acknowledged that "my work is my life."[6]

I've seen the difficulties firsthand. When I worked at a social services agency, many people were reluctant to take time off for fear that they would "get behind." A few of my clients have worked in organizations that made no allowance for people to take off the time to which they were entitled; the "missed" work had to be made up in the evenings and on weekends. The temptation can be to always keep going.

It's not just employees who don't feel like they have enough personal time. Women with kids especially tend to neglect personal time, relationship time, and sleep. In one study, for example, women were twice as likely as men to feel exhausted (15.7 vs. 8.7%).[7] Over half of all working parents find it difficult or impossible to juggle work and family responsibilities. For them, personal time is rarely in the equation.[8]

Why We Need Rest

We pay a price for our reluctance (or inability) to take a break. When you work for long periods, your ability to concentrate and remember decreases. Even brief scheduled breaks during the day to move or stretch help learning and memory significantly. A study by Atsunori Ariga and Alejandro Lleras, researchers at the University of Illinois at Urbana-Champaign, found that actively taking breaks improved both *attention* and *performance*.[9]

We talked in Chapter 6 about people's reluctance to schedule downtime. In many circles, working long hours is a sign of commitment, a badge of honor. A 12-hour day is seen as something to brag about. However, it's not a very effective way to work. Psychologist K. Anders Ericsson has studied elite performers for decades – authors, musicians, athletes, and others. His research shows that periods of rest are essential for good performance, and that rest is much more important than vacation time. For tasks that require concentration, he has found that it's most effective to work in stretches of 60-90 minutes and for no more than 5 hours a day.[10]

There's much more to Ericsson's research on performance, including what he calls "deliberate practice." What's relevant here is that his investigations show that high skill and productivity require rest. Without breaks in the day, the week, and the year, performance drops.

Exercise 10.5

a. Have you ever skipped breaks, worked through lunch, given up weekends, or skipped a vacation because you had too much work to do?

b. Where in your day can you take some time out to relax and renew your energy? When in the cycle of a year do you pause for time away from whatever it is that you consider work?

Celebrating with Others

Celebrating in relationship builds energy, helps people connect, and provides positive feedback. As a result, it brings people closer, according to researcher Shelly L. Gable and her colleagues at the University of California, Los Angeles and the University of Rochester.[11] Sharing positive events with someone you care about allows you to not only recreate the positive feeling that was part of the event, but also builds a sense of connection between you and your partner, colleague, or friend.

Dacher Keltner, in his book *Born to Be Good*, argues that positive relationships help us feel better about *ourselves*. In general, how connected we feel to other people affects our own sense of meaning in life. He describes how increasing the ratio of our positive to negative interactions with others increases our sense of well-being.[12]

Celebrating our success with others can help increase the number of positive interactions we share, by providing an opportunity to get positive feedback. This in turn can improve productivity. For example, researcher Marcial Losada says that for high-performing teams in business, the ratio of positive to negative feedback is 5.6 to 1. For low-performing teams, the ratio is 0.36 to 1. High-performing teams get greater than 15 times more positive feedback.[13]

Positive feedback from your partner is just as important. Marriage researcher John Gottman found that the balance is similar for couples. Couples who feel happy with their marriages have at least seven positive interactions for every negative one.[14]

If positive feedback isn't already a part of the culture where you work, you might be able to help create it. My client Alexi created a Friday afternoon tea to help celebrate the accomplishments of the week with her staff. The reward was not only tangible – the tea and snacks – but also intangible. During this time, each person shared an accomplishment or "win" for the week. In this way, each person helped inspire the others.

Cory found a way to give himself positive feedback by paying attention to the successful interactions he had with other people. Each day he acknowledged his own success by writing down his favorite encounter with someone at work, and what he liked about it. Each day for a month he was able to *notice* his success in reaching out and feel good about it. As a side benefit, his attention to those daily encounters helped him feel more connected with the people with whom he worked.

Exercise 10.6

Where do you get positive feedback for what you do? How could you encourage more positive feedback in your work or home life?

Exercise 10.7

a. *What do you need to celebrate?*

b. *Look through the list of celebrations at the end of this chapter, and choose a tiny celebration you can use to reward yourself for tiny successes.*

c. *Choose or invent at least one small celebration that will energize you at the end of your day.*

d. *Choose or invent at least one larger celebration you can use when you reach a more significant milestone, which could be a major event, or just the end of your week. When will it happen? Take a few minutes and write it on your calendar.*

It's worth celebrating every day. Simple celebrations encourage change, reinforce habits, provide inspiration, and make progress visible. In addition, celebration makes us happier and helps us to do well. Learning to appreciate the small, positive moments in your days will help move you, little by little, toward your goals.

Used in this way, celebration helps you focus on *the journey,* rather than postponing your reward until the big end result. As Mae West said, "You only live once, but if you do it right, once is enough." Celebration helps create a life worth living.

Key Points

+ Celebrating what's going well encourages more of it.

+ Reward is a key part of creating and reinforcing new habits.

+ Celebration makes the progress toward your goal visible, which inspires you to keep moving toward it.

+ Positive feedback improves performance and relationships, and therefore helps you meet your goals.

Simple Actions to Use for Celebrating

The possibilities for celebration are endless. The suggestions below are designed to inspire you to think of more ways on your own. Almost anything that provides rest, movement, social connection, or fun can be used as a celebration. Since the most common reasons people don't celebrate are time and cost, I've included micro-celebrations that cost nothing and take less than a minute, along with small and mid-sized celebrations (the big ones you can think of yourself). No excuses. Celebrate!

Micro-Celebrations

+ Smile.

+ Look out a window and appreciate the world's natural beauty.

+ Compliment yourself.

+ Congratulate yourself.

+ Tell yourself, "Yea me!"

- ✦ Highlight a completed task.
- ✦ Hug yourself.
- ✦ Let out a "whoop!"
- ✦ Jump up and down with delight.
- ✦ Dance across the room.

Small Celebrations

- ✦ Listen to a few minutes of relaxing music.
- ✦ Daydream.
- ✦ Take a walk.
- ✦ Sit down and kick your feet up.
- ✦ Light a candle and watch it flicker.
- ✦ Read a poem that inspires you.
- ✦ Step outside and stretch.
- ✦ Share your success with someone you care about.
- ✦ Take a few minutes to look at a favorite photo.
- ✦ Text a friend.
- ✦ Read something funny and laugh.
- ✦ Sing just for the fun of it.
- ✦ Have a bite of chocolate.
- ✦ Enjoy a slice of a crisp, green apple.
- ✦ Enjoy an ice cream cone.
- ✦ Have a cup of tea.

Mid-Sized Celebrations

- ✦ Take a walk in the park.
- ✦ Pick a bouquet of flowers from your yard and arrange them in a vase.

- Stroll through your neighborhood.
- Enjoy a nap.
- Soak in a hot bath.
- Watch the sunset.
- Schedule a day off to relax.
- Write down the three most important things that you accomplished today.
- Write about something you're proud of or grateful for.
- Brag to a friend.
- Watch something funny.
- Take a walk in the rain – with an umbrella or not!
- Make some chocolate chip cookies.
- Watch a movie with a friend.
- Visit an amusement park and go on your favorite rides.
- Go to a park to ride a swing and slide down a slide.
- Make a picnic and enjoy it on your patio.
- Plant some snapdragons.
- Watch your favorite movie.
- Make some popcorn.
- Snuggle up with a good novel.
- Play a game of *Monopoly*.
- Arrange a Friday night potluck.
- Fly a kite on the beach.

Conclusion

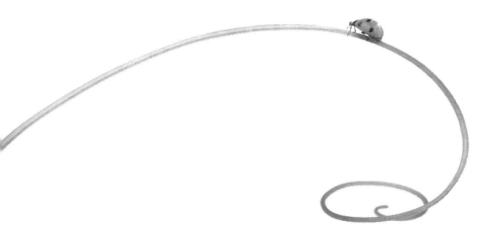

Expect the Impossible:
Small Change as a Way of Life

"People think that you have to do something huge,
like go to Africa and build a school, but you can make a small change
in a day. If you change Wednesday, then you change Thursday. Pretty soon
it's a week, then a month, then a year. It's bite-size, as opposed to feeling
like you have to turn your life inside-out to make changes."

– Hoda Kotb

It's powerful to dream big. Few worthwhile discoveries or accomplishments would have occurred without a big vision to guide them. However, every great change is made up of many small changes. That's what this book has been all about.

I believe that it's possible for you to create a life that is fulfilling and rewarding. In order to help with that endeavor, I've shared everything I know about creating real and lasting change: the science, examples of what my clients have accomplished, and suggestions for how to use the same strategies in your own life.

Now let's look at what happened to the three people you met in Chapter 1: Alexi, Cory, and Sandra. Through the process outlined in *Small Change, Big Results*, they each accomplished things that might have seemed impossible at first. Here is where they ended up.

The Stories: Part 2

Alex started by pausing to make room to renew her energy and gain perspective. That change in perspective led to changes in her attitude, mindset, and ultimately her actions. About a year after we started working together, Alexi was not only back on track financially, but she could even retire early if that was her choice. She expanded the 10 minutes of morning quiet time to a half an hour. Her evenings and weekends were free to spend with friends or enjoy time for herself. Her vision evolved as she continued to imagine how she wanted to live.

Alexi developed routines and habits to contain the randomness in her day. As a result, her focus improved. She was able, with the help of her physician, to stop the medication she had relied on for over a year. By making one small change at a time, she was able to not only create the business she dreamed about, but also begin to imagine the legacy she wanted to leave in the world and in her community.

Cory's changes also started small, but in six months he felt significantly calmer, and he could respectfully hold his ground even in difficult conversations. As he became more sure of himself, and more adept at understanding other people's agendas, he was better able to both put forth his point of view, and to listen and compromise. Cory not only kept his job, but a year later was offered a promotion. This was something Cory couldn't have imagined, let alone predicted, when we first started working together. As each small change led to another, Cory shifted not only his actions, but the way he thought about other people and himself.

You'll remember that Sandra's first small change was a daily 10-minute walk with her husband. This simple action grew into all-day adventures and other types of unpressured family time. As her communication with Jay improved, the two of them focused on restructuring their business. They developed a solid plan and agreed on their respective roles. As they got better at working together, Sandra and Jay started seeing each other as allies instead of critics. It was about two years before their business and their marriage were both going well. Four years after that, they're still happily married, and Sandra has started her own business in graphic design.

Many people, including folks like Alexi, Cory, and Sandra, have used the strategies presented here with amazing results. In these pages, there are, in fact, many examples to draw from, but every situation is unique. Each step in the process of change can be approached in several different ways. Try some of the ideas in each chapter, and choose the ones that work best for you. Remember that you'll probably run into obstacles, and you will almost certainly get sidetracked from time to time. When these things happen, you can either:

+ Use the strategies in this book to regroup and get back on track.
+ Get help.

Where to Apply the Principles of *Small Change, Big Results*

Below are some of the things you can accomplish by following the process described in this book.

Work and Productivity

+ Increase your income dramatically
+ Find a job you love
+ Start your own business
+ Get more done in your day
+ Improve your work-life balance

Relationships

+ Rekindle love
+ Spend time with people you care about
+ Build positive relationships with your partner, family, children, colleagues, and friends
+ Recover from a difficult event or situation

Health

+ Improve your physical health through fitness and eating well

+ Stop problem behaviors such as smoking and emotional eating

+ Stay focused and mentally sharp

+ Cultivate a sense of emotional balance, well-being, and inner peace

Contribution

+ Create a legacy you're proud of

+ Serve as an example of well-being and balance to your family and community

+ Balance service with responsibility and self-care

Looking Back – A Recap

At this point, you have all the ingredients and a process for bringing about simple, purposeful change. The skills you have learned can help you not only make positive, individual changes, but also can become a way of life. Using simple actions to make positive change can become the foundation of a healthy, positive approach to all of life's ups and downs, as well as a way to increase your productivity, build rewarding relationships, and enjoy your success. Let's take a few moments to consider how we got to this place.

We started by looking at the scope of change, how it can seem daunting at first, and how every "big" change is really built from a series of smaller steps. In Chapter 2, we looked at why attempts to change often fail despite our desire to make them happen. In Chapter 3, we discussed how the brain works with respect to change – how it's a flexible, resilient organ with an innate capacity for change.

In Part II, we looked at powerful tools for creating lasting change, with a focus on the concept of making change smaller. Any task or challenge can be broken down into simple, do-able steps. These steps were then arranged into a logical, easy-to-follow order. The process begins with a *Pause*. The first key to change is to take time out to consider where you've been and where you're going. In addition, you need to take the time to pause to help yourself relax, reflect, and think through what is meaningful and important to you. There are many ways to *pause*, and some are shared at the end of Chapter 4.

Next, in Chapter 5, we focused on finding inspiration for change through imagining. Your imagination and the ability to create a vision of a desired outcome are vital to the process of successful change. Commitment to your vision is also crucial, for it's all too easy to give up when things don't work out immediately. Creating a clear, compelling, positive vision sets the stage for that commitment, and thus for action you can sustain. It's important to both keep your vision realistic and at the same time be willing to stretch yourself and operate outside your comfort zone.

A vision without a plan is just a dream. It's fun to imagine something new, but even more exciting when you can bring your vision to life. In Chapter 6 ("Plan"), we looked at three ways to map out change: (1) choosing a next step, (2) working backward from the end, and (3) mind-mapping the possible steps. We looked at creating milestones and also reviewed the importance of having a plan that's realistic as well as challenging.

Small change is at the heart of this process, and it is described in Chapter 7, "Shrink." Small actions can bring about enormous changes in individuals, families, and organizations. Whether the problem is with a relationship, a career, a personal roadblock, or learning a new skill or activity, big changes have simple origins. Especially when life feels busy, stressful, or overwhelming, the key is to shrink your change into simple actions that seem easy, do-able, and even fun!

Everything described so far has been about *preparing* to act. Shifts in the way you *think* about change help create new habits and routines in our enormously flexible but routine-following brains. In Chapter 8

("Act"), we found that action is about consistency – doing something regularly until it becomes automatic. When actions are small and part of your routine, you don't have to wait for inspiration to strike or to be in the mood. When you create habits and a supportive environment, then you're more likely to continue moving forward and making change stick. Lastly, if you're struggling on your own, ask for help! Collaborate with a friend or partner. Seek the advice of a professional. Your present and future success and happiness are too important to abandon when things don't go smoothly!

Chapter 9, "Flow," focused on overcoming obstacles. This chapter outlined several strategies for *flowing* past them and keeping your momentum going. These involve changing the way you look at obstacles, and adjusting old ways of thinking. Instead of focusing on failure, for example, you can "experiment." In science and in life, not all experiments are successful, but each one is an opportunity to learn. Creating a different story about things that don't work, or sometimes changing your very thoughts, can bring excitement, comfort, and satisfaction to the process.

In Chapter 10, we focused on celebration, an often-overlooked part of the process of change. It's important to recognize progress, enjoy victories, and relish the positive things taking place in our lives. Celebration reinforces new habits, inspires action, and just feels good.

Celebrations are powerful, yet they too can be small. Taking a few moments to acknowledge a win can help you recognize and enjoy each incremental step toward our larger vision. Celebration builds momentum, and it deepens your connections with others. It brings energy, a lightened mood, and a promise of future success. In the final chapter, I share many ways to celebrate, from 10-second affirmations to all-day events. If a new action feels good, you'll keep doing it!

The *Small Change, Big Results* Post-Test

The purpose of this book is to help you understand the process – and the power – of small change, so that you can be more productive, creative, and connected with the important people in your life. So let's look at how much progress you've made. In Chapter 3 ("How People Change"), I asked you to complete the following inventory. Let's try that again now.

Which of the following statements are true for you now that you've completed the book and are on your way to making significant change? Write them on your designated notepad or check them off in the *Small Change, Big Results Workbook*. Your answers will show you how far you've come, and they'll help you identify your next step in creating positive change.

Pause

- ✦ I build personal time into each week.
- ✦ I spend quality time with my family and friends.
- ✦ I leave my work at work.
- ✦ I get enough sleep.
- ✦ I get enough exercise.
- ✦ I plan time each week for rest and renewal, in the form of mindfulness, inspirational reading, meditation, yoga, walks in nature, a spiritual practice, or another method of my choosing.

Imagine

- ✦ I understand the role of imagination in creating change.
- ✦ I'm clear about my top four or five values.
- ✦ Based on those values, I am able to create a vision that feels powerful and inspiring.

+ I've given my vision form (a written page, poster, or other reminder), so I can refer to it often.

Plan

+ I've selected one part of my vision to be my first goal.

+ I know the major steps I need to take in order to reach my goal.

+ I know how to break down those steps into smaller steps so I can clearly see when I'm making progress.

+ I understand how to use target dates to help myself stay on track with my goals.

+ I take time each day to plan, so that I schedule plenty of time for each task I need to complete.

Shrink

+ I understand the value of making small change.

+ I know how to shrink my actions until they feel simple and easy.

+ When I feel resistance, I make the task even easier.

Act

+ I know how to create routines so that follow-through on my commitments becomes automatic.

+ I know how to create an environment that makes taking action easy.

+ I'm willing to ask for help when I need it.

Flow

+ I'm comfortable with challenges; I see them as opportunities to stretch myself.

+ I understand that failure is a possible path to making significant accomplishments.

+ I'm willing to talk with people I trust about mistakes and wrong guesses, because I know that this moves me more quickly toward success.

+ I understand the power of stories, and I use them to inspire myself.

+ I know how to change negative, self-sabotaging thoughts into thoughts that are truthful but encouraging.

+ I nurture my own creativity so I can find unusual solutions to important problems.

Celebrate

+ I regularly celebrate my success.

+ I understand the power of gratitude in creating change.

+ I build time into my day and week for rest and renewal.

+ I use small rewards to help myself keep moving forward.

How does your total score now compare to your total score at the start of the book? Did the totals for any sections increase after working through the suggestions in this book? If you've made any progress at all, congratulations! Take a few minutes to celebrate!

Understanding is the first step. Now I'd like to invite you to create your own lasting change. Whether your desired change is currently large or small, personal or professional, within you or between you and someone else, you have the tools and skills to make it happen.

There's no single right way to start. Choose one small action, and use that to propel yourself into the next small action. Then pass your knowledge on to others. Let them know what you're doing, tell them about this book, and get them involved in their own change!

A Special Note to You
from the Author

I'd love to hear your story! Feel free to contact me and let me know about the changes you make. My contact information, qualifications, and services are listed in the back of the book. Thank you for sharing your valuable time with me.

www.smallchangebigresults.com/book
Pat@LaDouceurMFT.com

Endnotes

Chapter 1

1   Lehrer, Jonah. "Blame It on the Brain: The Latest Neuroscience Research Suggests Spreading Resolutions Out Over Time Is the Best Approach." *Wall Street Journal*, 2009.

2   Centers for Disease Control and Prevention. "Stress… At Work," NIOSH (National Institute for Occupational Safety and Health) Publication 99-101, http://www.cdc.gov/niosh/docs/99-101/.

3   Everest College Third Annual Survey. "Workplace Stress on the Rise: With 83% of Americans Frazzled by Something at Work," Globe Newswire, April 9, 2013 press release, http://globenewswire.com/news-release/2013/04/09/536945/10027728/en/Workplace-Stress-on-the-Rise-With-83-of-Americans-Frazzled-by-Something-at-Work.html.

Chapter 2

1   Lehrer, Jonah. "Blame It on the Brain: The Latest Neuroscience Research Suggests Spreading Resolutions Out Over Time Is the Best Approach." *Wall Street Journal*, http://online.wsj.com/news/articles/SB10001424052748703478704574612052322122442, December 26, 2009.

2   Schwartz, Tony, and Jean Gomes. *The Way We're Working Isn't Working: The Four Forgotten Needs that Energize Great Performance*. New York: Free Press, 2010.

3   Zimbardo, Philip G., and John Boyd. *The Time Paradox: The New Psychology of Time That Will Change Your Life*. New York: Free Press, 2008.

4   Baumeister, Roy F., and John Tierney. *Willpower: Rediscovering the Greatest Human Strength*. New York: Penguin Press, 2011.

5   McGonigal, Kelly. *The Willpower Instinct: How Self-Control Works, Why It Matters, and What You Can Do to Get More of It*. New York: Avery, 2012.

6   Niewenhuis, Loreen. *A 1000-Mile Walk on the Beach: One Woman's Trek of the Perimeter of Lake Michigan*: Crickhollow Books, 2011.

7   Gladwell, Malcolm. *Outliers: The Story of Success*. New York: Little, Brown and Co., 2008.

Chapter 3

1   Porter, Kay and Judy Foster. *Visual Athletics.* Dubuque, Iowa: William C. Publishers, 1990.

2   Imagery is used in many areas. See, for example, Sanders, C.W., et. al. "Learning basic surgical skills with mental imagery: using the simulation centre in the mind." National Center for Biotechnology Information, http://www.ncbi.nlm.nih.gov/pubmed/18435713.

3   Kraus, Michael W., Cassy Huang, and Dacher Keltner. "Tactile Communication, Cooperation, and Performance: An Ethological Study of the NBA," http://socrates.berkeley.edu/~keltner/publications/kraus.huang.keltner.2010.pdf.

4   Fredrickson, Barbara. "Positive Emotions Broaden and Build," http://www.unc.edu/peplab/publications/Fredrickson_AESP_final.pdf.

5   Arden, John B. *Rewire Your Brain: Think Your Way to a Better Life.* Hoboken, N.J.: Wiley, 2010.

6   Woollett, Katherine, Hugo J. Spiers, and Eleanor A. Maguire. "Talent in the taxi: a model system for exploring expertise." *Philosophical Transactions of the Royal Society B: Biological Sciences* 364: 1407-1416, and Maguire, Eleanor A., Katherine Woollette, and Hugo J. Spiers. "London Taxi Drivers and Bus Drivers: A Structural MRI and Neuropsychological Analysis." *Philosophical Transactions of the Royal Society B: Biological Sciences* 16: 1091-1101.

7   Driemeyer Joenna, et. al. (2008) "Changes in Gray Matter Induced by Learning – Revisited." PLoS ONE 3(7): e2669, doi:10.1371/journal.pone.0002669.

8   Hanson, Rick, and Richard Mendius. *Buddha's Brain the Practical Neuroscience of Happiness, Love, & Wisdom.* Oakland, CA: New Harbinger Publications, 2009.

Chapter 4

1   Selye, Hans. *The stress of life.* New York: McGraw-Hill, 1956.

2   See, for example, www.ncbi.nlm.nih.gov/pmc/articles/PMC3584580/.

3   See, for example, www.umassmed.edu/Content.aspx?id=42426.

4   See, for example, http://greatergood.berkeley.edu/topic/mindfulness/definition.

5   Benson, Herbert. *The Relaxation Response.* New York: William Morrow and Company, Inc., 1975.

6   Rakel, David. "What Is the Relaxation Response?" ABC News. December 17, 2009.

7   Brown, Richard P., and Patricia L. Gerbarg. *The Healing Power of Breath: Simple Techniques to Reduce Stress and Anxiety, Enhance Concentration, and Balance Your Emotions.* Boston: Shambhala Publications, 2012.

8   Kabbat-Zinn, John. *Full-Catastrophe Living: Using the Wisdom of Your Body and Mind to Face Stress, Pain, and Illness.* New York: Delacorte Press, 1990.

9   Massachusetts General Hospital press release, "Mindfulness meditation training changes brain structure in 8 weeks," January 21, 2011, www.massgeneral.org/about/pressrelease. aspx?id=1329.

10   Mogilner, Cassie, Zoë Chance, and Michael I. Norton. "Giving Time Gives You Time." *Psychological Science*, February 21, 2012, http://www.people.hbs.edu/mnorton/mogilner%20 chance%20norton.pdf.

Chapter 5

1   For example, the Cleveland Clinic has found that guided imagery helps patients recover from medical procedures such as heart surgery by decreasing pain, strengthening the immune system, improving sleep, and shortening hospital stays. "Cleveland Clinic - Guided Imagery & Heart Surgery." Cleveland Clinic, http://my.clevelandclinic.org/heart/prevention/ emotional-health/stress-relaxation/guided-imagery-heart-surgery.aspx. Mental practice also helps musicians improve their musical performance: Lotze, M., G. Scheler, H.-R.M Tan, C. Braun, and N. Birbaumer. "The Musician's Brain: Functional Imaging of Amateurs and Professionals during Performance and Imagery." *NeuroImage*, 2003, 1817-829, January 1, 2003; and athletes build strength: Ranganathan, Vinoth K., Vlodek Siemionow, Jing Z. Liu, Vinod Sahgal, and Guang H. Yue. "From Mental Power to Muscle Power – Gaining Strength by Using the Mind." *Neuropsychologia* 42 (2004): 944-56.

2   Driskell, James E, Carolyn Copper, and Aidan Moran. "Does Mental Practice Enhance Performance?" *Journal of Applied Psychology*, August 1994, 79: 481-492, http://psycnet.apa. org/index.cfm?fa=buy.optionToBuy&id=1995-00363-001.

3   LotRProject, "An Analysis of Tolkien's Books: Word Count and Density," http:// lotrproject.com/statistics/books/wordscount.

4   Latham, Gary P., and Edwin A. Locke. "New Directions in Goal-Setting Theory." *Current Directions in Psychological Science*, 15: 265-268.

5   Statistic Brain, "Marathon Running Statistics." http://www.statisticbrain.com/marathon-running-statistics

6   Kruger, J., S.A. Ham, and H.W. Kohl. "Characteristics of a 'weekend warrior': results from two national surveys." *Medicine and Science in Sports and Exercise,* May 2007, 39(5): 796-800, http://www.ncbi.nlm.nih.gov/pubmed/17468576.

7   John F. Kennedy, address at Rice University on the nation's mission for space exploration, Houston, Texas, September 12, 1962.

Chapter 6

1   Rogers, Anne E. and Ronda Hughes (Ed.). "Chapter 40: The Effects of Fatigue and Sleepiness on Nurse Performance and Patient Safety." In *Patient Safety and Quality: An Evidence-Based Handbook for Nurses*. Rockville, MD: Agency for Healthcare Research and Quality, U.S. Dept. of Health and Human Services, 2008.

2   Caldwell, Ph.D., John A.. "Parallel Session: Operational Evidence of Fatigue – Flight Operations; Sleep and Psychomotor Performance during Commercial Ultra-Long-Range Flights." Lecture, FAA Fatigue Management Symposium: Partnerships for Solutions; Vienna, VA: June 17-19, 2008.

3   Perlow, Leslie A., and Jessica L. Porter. "Making Time Off Predictable – and Required." *Harvard Business Review,* October 2009; 87, 10.

4   Jackson, Dr. Thomas, and Sharman Lichtenstein. "Inefficient Use of Email Is Costing Business Plenty." Deakin University Australia's *Research Showcase*, May 11, 2011, originally in *International Journal of Internet and Enterprise Management,* www.deakin.edu.au/research/stories/2011/05/11/inefficient-use-of-email-is-costing-business-plenty.

5   Pattison, Kermit. "Worker, Interrupted: The Cost of Task Switching – Fast Interview with Gloria Mark, Professor, Department of Informatics, University of California, Irvine." *Fast Company,* July 28, 2008, http://www.fastcompany.com/944128/worker-interrupted-cost-task-switching.

6   Dominican University of California. "Study Backs Up Strategies for Achieving Goals: Psychology professor Dr. Gail Matthews has advice...," http://www.dominican.edu/dominicannews/study-backs-up-strategies-for-achieving-goals.

7   Statistic Brain. "New Years Resolution Statistics." Original source: University of Scranton, *Journal of Clinical Psychology.* http://www.statisticbrain.com/new-years-resolution-statistics.

8   "Presenteeism on the Rise as Employees Show Fatigue From a Slow- to No-Hire Economy." ComPsych. October 29, 2012. http://www.compsych.com/press-room/press-releases-2012/678-October-29-2012.

Chapter 7

1   Baumeister, Roy F., and Brad J. Bushman. *Social Psychology and Human Nature.* Belmont, CA: Thomson Higher Education, 2008.

2   Montez, J. K., and Debra Umberson. "Social Relationships and Health: A Flashpoint for Health Policy." *Journal of Health and Social Behavior,* 2010; 51(Suppl.), S54-S66, www.ncbi.nlm.nih.gov/pmc/articles/PMC3150158/.

3   Diener, Ed, Ed Sandvik, and William Pavot. "Happiness Is the Frequency, Not the Intensity, of Positive Versus Negative Affect." In *Assessing Well-Being: The Collected Works of Ed Diener.* Dordrecht: Springer, 2009.

4   Fredrickson, Barbara. *Love 2.0: Finding Happiness and Health in Moments of Connection.* New York: Plume, 2013.

5   McCullough, Michael E., and Robert A. Emmons. *"Counting Blessings Versus Burdens: An Experimental Investigation of Gratitude and Subjective Well-Being in Daily Life." Journal of Personality and Social Psychology 84,* No. 2: 377-389, http://greatergood.berkeley.edu/pdfs/GratitudePDFs/6Emmons-BlessingsBurdens.pdf.

Chapter 8

1   Duhigg, Charles. *The power of habit: why we do what we do in life and business.* New York: Random House, 2012.

2   Pressfield, Steven. *Turning Pro: Tap Your Inner Power and Create Your Life's Work.* New York: Black Irish Entertainment, May 31, 2012.

3   Kellogg School of Management. "The Power of Temptation: Professor Loran Nordgren finds that people believe they have more restraint than they actually possess." August 3, 2009. www.kellogg.northwestern.edu/news_articles/2009/nordgren_research.aspx.

4   Babcock, Linda, and Sara Laschever. *Women Don't Ask: Negotiation and the Gender Divide.* Princeton, N.J.: Princeton University Press, September 2, 2003.

Chapter 9

1   Jordan, Michael as quoted in *Nike Culture: The Sign of the Swoosh,* by Robert Goldman and Stephen Papson, (SAGE Publications, 1998), 49.

2   Rossman, Martin L. *The Worry Solution: Using Breakthrough Brain Science to Turn Stress and Anxiety into Confidence and Happiness.* New York: Crown Archetype, 2010.

3   Kostyanaya, Maria. "Can Stories Change the Brain?" *The Neuropsychotherapist,* January 12, 2014, www.neuropsychotherapist.com/can-stories-change-the-brain/.

4   Berns, Gregory S. et al. "Short- and Long-Term Effects of a Novel on Connectivity in the Brain," *Brain Connectivity,* 2013; 3, 6: 590-600.

5   MacDonald, J. Randall. "Working Beyond Borders: Insights from the Global Chief Human Resource Study," IBM, 2010, http://public.dhe.ibm.com/common/ssi/ecm/en/gbe03353usen/GBE03353USEN.PDF.

6   Howell, Elizabeth. "Apollo 13: Facts about NASA's Near-Disaster," Space.com, August 23, 2012, www.space.com/17250-apollo-13-facts.html.

7   Chaikin, Andrew. "Apollo 13 Astronauts Share Surprises from Their 'Successful Failure' Mission," Space.com, April 14, 2010, www.space.com/8215-apollo-13-astronauts-share-surprises-successful-failure-mission.html.

8   Dunbar, Brian. "Apollo 13," NASA, last updated September 19, 2013, www.nasa.gov/mission_pages/apollo/missions/apollo13.html#.U5udxyjig6x.

Chapter 10

1   Morse, Gardiner. "The Science Behind the Smile: An Interview with Daniel Gilbert," *Harvard Business Review,* January-February 2012.

2   Breuning, Ph.D., Loretta Graziano. *Meet Your Happy Chemicals.* Oakland, CA: System Integrity Press, 2012.

3   Culberson, Ron. *Do It Well. Make It Fun: The Key to Success in Life, Death, and Almost Everything in Between.* Austin, Texas: Greenleaf Book Group Press, 2012.

4   Yahoo Finance. "Staples Survey Reveals Many Employees Feel Too Guilty to Take Breaks, Despite Spending Longer Hours at Work," Staples Canada Press Release, May 7, 2014, http://finance.yahoo.com/news/staples-survey-reveals-many-employees-105700369.html.

5   Braverman, Samantha (Sr. Project Researcher). "Americans Work on Their Vacation: Half of those vacationing this summer will work on their vacation, including checking emails, voicemails and taking phone calls," Harris Interactive, July 28, 2011, www.harrisinteractive. com/NewsRoom/HarrisPolls/tabid/447/mid/1508/articleId/843/ctl/ReadCustom%20 Default/Default.aspx.

6   Expedia Vacation Deprivation Survey 2012, Harris Interactive, Banner Book #4, http://media.expedia.com/media/content/expus/graphics/other/pdf/Expedia-VacationDeprivation2012.pdf.

7   Centers for Disease Control and Prevention. "QuickStats: Percentage of Adults Who Often Felt Very Tired or Exhausted in the Past 3 Months, by Sex and Age Group - National Health Interview Survey, United States, 2010-2011." Centers for Disease Control and Prevention. http://www.cdc.gov/mmwr/preview/mmwrhtml/mm6214a5.htm?s_cid=mm6214a5_w.

8   Parker, Kim, and Wendy Wang. "Modern Parenthood." Pew Research Centers Social Demographic Trends Project RSS. http://www.pewsocialtrends.org/2013/03/14/modern-parenthood-roles-of-moms-and-dads-converge-as-they-balance-work-and-family/.

9   Lleras, Alejandro and Atsunori Ariga. "Brief and rare mental 'breaks' keep you focused: Deactivation and reactivation of task goals preempt vigilance decrements," *Cognition,* 2011, http://news.illinois.edu/WebsandThumbs/Lleras,Alejandro/Lleras_sdarticle-17.pdf.

10   Ericsson, K. Anders. "The Influence of Experience and Deliberate Practice on the Development of Superior Expert Performance." In *The Cambridge Handbook of Expertise and Expert Performance,* Chapter 38, http://www.skillteam.se/wp-content/uploads/2011/12/Ericsson_delib_pract.pdf.

11   Gable, Shelly L., et al. "What Do You Do When Things Go Right? The Intrapersonal and Interpersonal Benefits of Sharing Positive Events." *Journal of Personality and Social Psychology,* 87, 2: 228-245.

12   Keltner, Dacher. *Born to Be Good: The Science of a Meaningful Life*. New York: W.W. Norton & Co., 2009.

13   Losada, Marcial, and Emily Heaphy. "The Role of Positivity and Connectivity in the Performance of Business Teams: A Nonlinear Dynamics Model." *American Behavioral Scientist* 47: 740-765.

14   Gottman, John Mordechai, and Nan Silver. *Why Marriages Succeed or Fail and How You Can Make Yours Last*. New York: Simon & Schuster, 1995.

FREE Workbook Available Online!

Get a copy of the *Small Change, Big Results*
complimentary workbook (and *Small Gifts* newsletter) at
www.smallchangebigresults.com/book.

Additional Online Resources

Go to www.smallchangebigresults.com/resources/scbr
to learn more about books and other resources to
support a productive, stress-free lifestyle.

Speaking and Workshops

Dr. Pat LaDouceur leads programs and gives presentations for businesses, educational institutions, and private groups.
Topics are listed below. Training can be customized for your organization.

+ Facilitate effective teamwork

+ Manage stress and excel under pressure

+ Solve problems with creativity and ease

+ Become more confident and effective

+ Make the tasks you do each day relevant by linking them to a well-thought-out plan, and linking that plan to your *values*

+ Be a high performer at work while maintaining work/life balance

For more information or to request a talk or program,
contact Dr. LaDouceur at pat@ladouceurmft.com.

Counseling and Neurofeedback

What if you could DREAM BIG – and then had a simple, practical, step-by-step method to reach your goals? As a Psychotherapist and Board Certified Neurofeedback Practitioner, Pat LaDouceur works with private counseling and neurofeedback clients at her office in Albany, California. She also offers short-term, focused coaching for professionals, parents, and students across the country.

www.smallchangebigresults.com/book
Pat@LaDouceurMFT.com
510-277-0456

*"Big changes have small origins.
Small actions help get you started,
and getting started is the key
to getting things done."*

– Pat LaDouceur

18100745R00112

Made in the USA
San Bernardino, CA
29 December 2014